HEART AND HOME:

Rooms that Tell Stories

Linda O'Keeffe

RIZZOLI
NEW YORK

New York · Paris · London · Milan

First published in the United States
of America in 2014 by
Rizzoli International Publications, Inc.
300 Park Avenue South
New York, NY 10010
www.rizzoliusa.com

ISBN: 978-0-8478-4364-0
LCCN: 2014939605

© 2014 Linda O'Keeffe

Designed by Claudia Brandenburg

Printed and bound in China

2014 2015 2016 2017 2018 / 10 9 8 7 6 5 4 3 2 1

INTRODUCTION

A home is much more than a dwelling, place of birth, or primary residence. It's an earnest evocation, an aching for safety, a longing for peace in a primal, political, and poetical sense. It's wherever we feel creative or relaxed enough to permanently loosen our stays. It's a stage for "life's undress rehearsal." It's where we hang our hat and park our heart. Whether our childhood home resembled a palace, playground, or prison, as our primary universe it's the underpinning of our aesthetic identity. "Over and beyond our memories, the house we were born in is physically inscribed in us," writes Gaston Bachelard. "It is a group of organic habits." It defined harmony for us even if it offered up dysfunction. It gave us our first glimpses of light, shape, and texture; it introduced us to concepts of depth, order, and composition; it gave us our spatial awareness and it showed us the power of color. On the winding road to personal-izing our taste maybe we'll emulate or rebel against all of those early perceptions. Maybe we'll tweak, twist, affectionately pervert, enshrine, refine, or totally dismiss them. Maybe we'll parody them or serve them up with an added dose of irony, but as our visual mother tongue they're with us for life. The reason we can never go back home is because we never actually left.

By osmosis our parents' things—their knickknacks, curtains, clothing, cutlery, cars, furni-ture, tools, wallpaper, and bathroom tiles—define a notion of comfort that thrills us, irks us, or leaves us cold. Snarky couturiers define comfort as a plebian preoccupation with tent dresses, sweat pants, and orthopedic shoes, but top interior designers think of it as a necessary luxury. Their ideal scenario is for every client to walk into a newly installed room and say, "I feel as if I've always lived here." The inference is clear—"I feel pampered and secure enough here to utterly be myself." Every aspect of an interior's decor is subjective but none more so than color, which is why red walls may relax one person while they agitate another, and why white may feel cleansing and meditative or sterile and cold.

One man's kitsch may well be another man's chic, but experiencing a sense of well being when we're in the midst of things we love is a universal, cross cultural truth. Anyone who lives with tons of possessions is easily disparaged as materialistic while anyone who lives with con-spicuous austerity and restraint seems to know "you can't take it with you." But that polemic overlooks the therapeutic effect collecting, acquiring, and hunter-gathering has on the psyche. It ignores the impact belongings have on our emotional lives. As designer Ilse Craword once put it, "Long-held possessions are familiar faces, friends to hang out with when the going gets tough." Or as James Joyce expressed in loftier terms, "Any object, intensely regarded, may be a gate of access to the incorruptible eon of the gods." Our books are wells of knowledge and vehicles of escape and, like our children and pets, we miss them when we're away from them for too long. We relish our framed photographs for their solace and inspiration. A postcard of the Eiffel Tower prompts us to check out the price of a flight to Paris. A matchbook reminds us of the last time we had drinks with a former boyfriend. We trust our chairs to support us; we prefer one cappuccino cup to another.

Each person featured in this volume feels a strong affection for their possessions, and while most are avid consumers none is fettered to the material world. No one is driven to keep up with the Joneses by buying the latest and greatest, and no one equates the worth of his treasures with its monetary value. As Carey Maloney puts it, "It's how you spend, not how much." Scott Campbell believes the subtext in each photograph he owns enriches his inner life. Tom Pfeffer recalls feeling liberated when he was on a trip and lost his luggage, and an empty studio and the state of being without gives Christopher Kurtz perspective on whatever he subsequently sculpts. By constructing their seemingly disparate displays of patinated artifacts, Calvin Tsao and Zack McKown contemplate societal similarities and thereby tap into all of humanity.

Several people in these pages see themselves as stewards rather than owners of their worldly possessions, and many give preference to handmade rather than machine-made goods, so their paintings show the artist's brushstrokes or their asymmetrical chairs are evidently built from scratch. Hanya Yanagihara sees her loft as a receptacle for the love and creative talents that a particular group of artists and artisans invested in their work. Ronnie Schwartz refers to his furniture as characters, and Philip Michael Wolfson and Wolfgang Joop see their objects and companions in a similar light—they all have character, originality, and are fun to be around.

Shamir Shah and Rene Gonzalez are as attached to their designed objects as they are to the stones and seed pods they pick up while traveling. Ronald Bricke has as much of a relationship with the light in his apartment as he does with his museum-quality treasures. Paul Mathieu routinely gives away clothing he hasn't worn in six months and reduces his essential needs to pencil and paper, while John Jay defines home as "wherever your life story pieces together in the smallest details and the largest expressions." Like many of the people featured in the following pages, if David Serrano's Hollywood house went up in flames, from the thousands of clothing items, artwork, books, furniture, and pottery he owns, it would never occur to him to rescue any of these before his partner, Robert Willson, because ultimately he believes "things are just things." Objects may enhance our mood, notch up our level of contentment, promote a state of equilibrium, and bring about immeasurable amounts of joy but they're not a substitute for happiness.

When our chosen objects sooth us it's because they embody whatever narrative we project onto them. "My aunt gave me this vase," "I bought this stool at Porte de Vanves," "I love purple," "Gracie made this ceramic bird." Together the various meanings form a mise-en-scène where a powerful, nurturing atmosphere is as protective as the packing material used to stabilize a breakable inside a mailed carton. At the end of the day the colors we respond to and the objects we love reveal who we intrinsically are. They paint our portrait and write our biography.

ANTONIO PIO SARACINO

It's Nurturing to Be Alone in My Own Mind, I Mean, World

Antonio Pio Saracino's entire apartment is a viewing gallery, a 1,200-square-foot cabinet of curiosities. At every turn there's an award-winning photograph or a furniture prototype. "I collect a lot and I designed many of the things here and I suppose they're all quite attention grabbing," he says. "So when people first walk in here, curiosity gets the better of them and they sort of forget I'm here. Even when old friends come they discover something new about me." On one tiny section of a desk there's a mind-boggling number of items—a hand-painted turtle shell, a ceramic Herend deer, an eighteenth-century printing plate from Gustave Doré, Piranesi prints with overlapping graphics, an eighteenth-century alabaster reproduction of the *Spinario* from the Capitoline Museum in Rome, a scientific molecular model, and a reproduction of a Mies van der Rohe sketch. On the shelf above is an eighteenth-century reproduction of an Egyptian statue, the sculpted head of a mythical Satyrus, a few painted skulls, a stainless-steel model of the Atomium Pavilion in Brussels, a model of the moon covered by a Pulcinella mask, a pair of antlers, and fossilized dinosaur eggs. "As Nietzsche put it in *Beyond Good and Evil*, humans are the only animals who need objects to live in this world," says Saracino, "for their functionality and for their ability to convey a person's outlook on life. The things we choose to have around us express our wishes, transgressions, and dreams. They mirror our thoughts and organize our reality."

His snug condominium sits adjacent to the High Line on Manhattan's west side. "It's located close to hubs of cafés, cinemas, and art galleries, but I make sure to spend at least one night at home every week," he says. "I find it nurturing to be alone in my own mind, I mean, world." While its living room overlooks a high-traffic cross street, its kitchen window frames a postcard view of the Empire State Building, Renzo Piano's New York Times building, and Sir Norman Foster's Hearst Tower. "I can't think of a better place for an architect to have breakfast," he says. "I put the dining table in the center of the kitchen to remind me of my home in Puglia, because when I grew up during the 1980s and 1990s it was the family's 'hearth,' and it's still the center of interaction and social activity."

Saracino's father fed his son's emerging interest in art by giving him books, and his grandfather introduced him to architecture by teaching him how to cut out paper models of

Left: Saracino's library takes up an entire wall of the living room. A random layout of shelves, cubbyholes, and shadow boxes house books as well as a dizzying diversity of things he's collected or made. Miniature, three-dimensional models represent a handful of his award-winning, prototype chairs.

Facing page: In the living room, twenty circular lighting fixtures hug the ceiling. Saracino constructed a coffee table from bundled paper tubes whose caps he filled with blue and green ceramics. "Both designs echo each other and remind me of molecular structures," he says. Carved from high-density foam, his Ray chair is part of the permanent collection of New York's Museum of Arts and Design.

buildings his firm had developed. When Sarcino moved to Rome, he started to look at design in a historical context because its effect on the city's cultural evolution is so palpable. Many years later, as an assistant professor at the University of Rome, he was offered an internship in New York and once he arrived he decided not to leave. "It's one of the most integrated cities I know," he says, "and its cross-pollination of cultures is inspiring. It's a bridge to the rest of the world."

In his parents' house, alongside generic and classical furniture, every room had a central, gilt Murano glass chandelier. "The juxtaposition of the baroque and the utilitarian intrigued me. I thought how wonderful it would be if a single object conveyed emotional exuberance in a simple but eloquent way," he says. "Then I realized how nature does that all the time, and that's when I began using algorithms to convey that sense in my designs."

Saracino wants to make distinctive furniture and architecture, but he's careful not to overthink their design and finds it soul destroying when an object's sole raison d'être is its uniqueness. "At heart people in my profession are optimists. We have a desire to enhance life or to improve something that already exists, so cynicism and anger don't fit into the equation," he says, "which is why my approach is to be playful and curious." On his way home one evening he found an abandoned reproduction of the iconic Red Blue chair Gerrit Rietveld designed in 1918 as an homage to Piet Mondrian. Saracino drew wavy force field lines across its seat and back to imply a reclining human body. "It was my attempt to illustrate how energy is inherent to the most inanimate of objects."

Saracino's upholstery and walls are a limited range of grays and blues. In his furniture he sometimes uses bright reds and oranges as a flare to draw the eye inward or outward, but he can only live with cool colors. "They balance my mood and my personality which have a tendency to be warm and a bit fiery," he says. "Like everything, it's a symbiotic relationship."

Left: In the dining area of the kitchen a Rietveld chair sits next to a wine rack and a steel model of the Empire State Building, which is located a few blocks from the apartment. The rubber King Kong and the Greek bust, its chest emblazoned with a Superman logo, are quick illustrations of Saracino's humor. The wall-mounted light box displays an ocean view of his hometown of Puglia.

Facing page: Deep blue walls bookend the all-white kitchen and dining area originating at the apartment's entrance. The variation in the venation of Saracino's Leaf chair corresponds to ergonomics. Lighting gadgetry in the ceiling projects the word "yes" onto a stainless steel ball on a console and serves as a daily reminder of American optimism.

Right: Saracino is an accomplished chef, and his limited-edition Lampo chandelier provides the main light source for the dinner parties he often hosts. Surrounded by Herman Miller chairs, a terrarium and a Pythagoras bowl he constructed from recycled cardboard sit centrally on a glass table. A salon-style arrangement of artwork depicts various Italian rural scenes and provides the room with its main focal point.

Overleaf: Panels upholstered with gray linen extend the headboard, align with a desk alcove, and impose an architectural horizontality in the bedroom. An eighteenth-century bronze statue of a wolf inspired Saracino's photograph, titled *Mother's Instinct*.

Partners Brian McCarthy and Danny Sagar refer to the architectural style of their Kerhonkson, New York, weekend house as "midwestern Greek Revival" and its interior decor as "scrapbook" and "non-deliberate." In the entry hall a painting by Chris Doyle hangs above a nineteenth-century North African table, where a mannequin torso by John Sidell sits on top of a late-eighteenth-century sculpture stand.

BRIAN McCARTHY

This House Didn't Spring Forth from a Shopping List

If Brian McCarthy had to pick a common factor in each of his favorite interiors it would be their rich, strong voice. "I'm a decorator in every sense of the word," he says, "and surface tactility is one of my strongest suits so I like rooms that are cohesive and make a definitive statement." Whether it's an ambassadorial residence in London or a private hammam in Gstaad, all of his projects have the finely tuned multilayering that stems from an inspired, creatively unfettered master plan. Details in recent commissions include a ceiling inspired by a Tiepolo fresco, a four-poster bed constructed entirely out of bronze, an appliquéd leather curtain inspired by an Alexander McQueen gown, a bedroom wall inlaid with pheasant feathers, furrows of polished agate set into spruce paneling, and a "crazy, mad Regency-style room with Chinese lacquer and paneled mirrors. The kind of budgets my clients are lucky enough to have allows for a lot of fantasy and I embrace that. The fact that I also get to rub shoulders with talented artisans and craftspeople who produce masterful work is an added bonus. I mean, what better life could there be?"

The grandeur and scale of his projects may vary, but his initial approach is always the same. "It starts with the architecture and as I process space three dimensionally my first walk through almost feels cinematic," he says, "and as I go from room to room I'm considering function and weighing up the available light before I establish a color scheme." After he's drawn up a scaled plan he layers surface materials, art, furniture, and objects on top of color and keeps honing until every view from every vantage point feels resolved. "I spin the plan around and put myself in every seat and imagine all the perspectives. Every view has to be considered and resolved."

McCarthy grew up in Bethesda, Maryland, in the 1930s Tudor-style stucco and stone house his parents still own. "They've traveled a lot, extensively in Asia, so the rooms are peppered with Danish modern furniture, objects from China, Korea, and Japan, and carpets from Uzbekistan and Morocco. It's layered like a nomadic scrapbook. Their adventurousness left a long-lasting impression on me because I was exposed to so many different cultures and customs."

His grandmother's house in Georgia cultivated his appetite for oversized, formal spaces. "It was grand and it lived large," he recalls, "with dark wraparound porches, a central hallway, a stately paneled library, and a proper living room with eighteenth-century antiques,

Clockwise from top left: "I'm a fan of classical structure," says McCarthy, "but here Danny and I went for softened edges, and any precious pieces we own fly under the radar." In the living room, a seventeenth-century Louis XIV chair with a ratcheted back is paired with an early-nineteenth-century Dutch pedestal and an oversize pinecone urn they picked up locally.

In the master bedroom, linen jacquard curtains frame a backlit early-nineteenth-century Empire chair.

To the right of the living room fireplace a stool, drinks table, floor lamp, and pedestal surround a tufted velvet armchair, all acquired from places as geographically diverse as the Clignancourt flea market and the Rhinebeck Antiques Fair.

Right: A collection of art on the second-floor landing centers around a gesso and gilded-wood Emilio Terry–style console. Above it hangs Sze Tsung Leong's photograph *Tiananmen Square, Beijing, 2002*, adjacent to an untitled photograph by Heimo Zobernig. Sagar's collection of wire objects crops up throughout the house and includes Thai Varick's horse sculpture.

and I was fascinated by the comings and goings in the kitchen and butler's pantry." He earned a bachelor of fine arts in interior design at the Pratt Institute in the early 1980s and immediately joined the prestigious firm of Parish-Hadley, where he rapidly ascended and became a partner within six years.

In the weekend house he shares with his partner, Danny Sagar, in upstate New York the scale is semi-grand—the spacious living room has ten-foot-high ceilings and occupies most of the ground floor. It looks out onto a deep terrace and five acres landscaped according to McCarthy's sketches with undulating boxwoods, beds of ornamental grasses, stocky hydrangea bushes, and dozens of Heritage birch trees. The garden's formality is offset by the house's consciously casual vibe. "A lot of people in our profession are overly self-conscious about how they live," says Sagar, who manages McCarthy's firm, "but we wanted this space to feel intimate and welcoming, to have heart and soul, which means it's constantly evolving. It didn't spring fully formed from a shopping list."

Despite or maybe due to a travel schedule that can easily see him taking international flights a few times a week, McCarthy's essentially a homebody happy to mix himself a gimlet at the end of the day and watch the TV news. "Natural beauty is my biggest inspiration," he says, "so I spend as much time as I can here where I have access to gardening and horse riding on a friend's farm because I need the equilibrium, I need to keep my head sane and level. Besides, my life inspires my work."

McCarthy believes color and art provide the heartbeat of a room, and early on in his career Impressionism and Cubism opened his eyes to abstract and then Conceptual art. "Becoming aware of the progression of history was important for me. It made me appreciate the context of things more and made me realize that I have a tremendous tolerance for all periods and styles of furniture and art. Except maybe Edwardian Victorian," he says. "Some heavy, oppressive pieces from that era literally suck the lifeblood out of a room."

Below: A sizable eighteenth-century French mahogany desk occupying a slice of the spacious master bedroom is positioned beneath photographs by Lise Sarfati and Elisabetta Benassi. The table lamp is by Tom Blake; the chair to the left is an eighteenth-century, Louis XVI fauteuil de bureau and its opposite is a gilded wood Empire bergère from the 1820s. In the corner, the crystalline glazed pot on the eighteenth-century pedestal is by ceramicist Kate Malone.

Right: The dining table is situated at one end of the living room in close proximity to the kitchen; seated guests look directly onto a garden and surrounding acreage that was formally uncultivated alfalfa fields as far as the eye could see. Whether it's Herve van der Straeten's wall sconces, Erik Eiserling's center-piece glass bowl, or the Gustavian chest of drawers, McCarthy and Sagar know exactly when and where they obtained each one of their belongings.

Overleaf: To the left of the entrance into the living room, a huge canvas by Kati Heck, entitled *Spring Cleaning*, epitomizes the wit and stylistic blend in the house's formal and familiar decor. A backgammon table supports an iron and natural sponge table lamp designed by Hélène de Saint Leger and sidles up to a late-eighteenth-century Directoire daybed. McCarthy remembers wrestling the piece away from Sister Parish when they were on a Manhattan shopping spree together more than twenty-five years ago. "She was ready to knock my lights out, but I saw it first!"

A Dictogrand radio loudspeaker from the 1920s and a robust wrought iron coat stand flank a cabinet of curios in the common area in Calvin Tsao and Zack McKown's former Soho design studio. The cast of characters also included an aluminum submarine sculpture from the 1930s, a George III Chippendale armchair, two paper wasps' nests, and a pair of high-heeled shoes designed by Rei Kawakubo. "When Calvin first set them out as objects I didn't know what possessed him," says McKown, "but I've grown to think of them as the ruby slippers remade in black rubber."

CALVIN TSAO & ZACK McKOWN

Roles and Rules for the Decorative and Whimsical

Zack McKown is drawn to nineteenth-century cabinet pulls. He also has a soft spot for plumbing fixtures, particularly the generic, non-attention-grabbing kind. "They do what they're supposed to do so they're honest and innocent," he says, "and the great thing about innocence is that it can't be consciously adopted. It just is!" Then there's his "weird science" Geophone stethoscope, whose sole raison d'être is to detect underground streams. And the tapered metal caber road builders use to pummel cobblestones. Then there's his minifleet of 1961 Lincolns: "As a child I desperately wanted to drive one but now that's not the point," he says. "I'm restoring them because they're historical artifacts." Calvin Tsao, his life and business partner, nods in agreement. "We're stewards," he says. "We're caretaking of all this paraphernalia and we'll make sure it all finds a suitable home when we kick the bucket."

The sedans and convertibles are garaged in a barn surrounded by apple orchards and woodlands on their upstate New York weekend property, but the bulk of the quirky, weathered artifacts they find at flea markets and auctions filled the reception area and lined the conference room of the studio they occupied until very recently on a spacious floor of a 1920s factory building in lower Manhattan. The groupings of furniture, lamps, display cases, framed artwork, shoes, cabinets, and mannequins seemed random but en masse they queried the intentionality of design. They illustrated how handsome and intriguing functionality can be. They were a testament to beauty's nonconformity. "There's a controlled scientific condition to aesthetics that's reliant on proportion and symmetry, but we don't assemble things solely for their superficial value," says Tsao. "We assemble for their history and for the sensibility behind their existence. They celebrate the commonality inherent in the disparate and the diverse, which is a metaphor for every aspect of our lives. So when you place an African stool alongside a gumball machine, a Louis XVII chair, and a wasp's nest, it's an indirect link to all of humanity."

Born in Hong Kong, Tsao hails from a family who led a nomadic life. His mother was cultured and took him to ballet, painting, violin, and calligraphy classes (where he repeatedly drew circles for three months), while his father cautioned against creative pursuits. "They can't feed you," he would say. "Every few years our family home underwent a radical cosmetic transformation and the ancestral artifacts my parents cherished and brought from China—

Facing page: In the reception area an air of conventional practicality projected by a Jean Prouve desk, a 1950s Alvar Aalto lamp, and a plywood screen designed by Charles Eames in 1946 was offset by a mid-century metal globe that converts into a cocktail bar, a spouted pot once used for smelting iron ore, a Chinese medicine ball, and a vitrine of seashells.

Right: In one corner of the reception space a handsome library card file designed by Jens Risom was paired with a nineteenth-century firemen's ladder, while a set of 1950s cast aluminum head moulds, once used to form rubber masks, had the fractured perspective of a Francis Bacon triptych. "Some things are designed to be intentionally beautiful," says Tsao, "and some things are beautiful despite the intention of their maker."

a Ming dynasty chair and a few brush pots—always had pride of place," says Tsao, "but they seldom related to my mother's decorating themes. There was a disconnection."

McKown grew up in South Carolina, and his mother had a strong appreciation for craft and texture as well as the ability to integrate her surroundings. With inspiration from a Frank Lloyd Wright project and no formal training, she reclaimed the house's unfinished basement. When McKown was five or six he remembers her telling a carpenter to take down the cabinets he'd just built. "She was on a tight budget," he remembers, "but couldn't live with something that was compositionally wrong, and that really affected me." In his freshman year of high school he arguably appropriated her ingenuity, and with his father's encouragement and the help of a local contractor, he designed and built a one-room summerhouse out of polyurethane foam with parabolic openings on two ends, which became his portfolio for architecture school.

Since they first met in 1976 at Harvard during an animated scrap over desk space, their individual differences have formed their common ground. "We amplify each other's strengths and cover each other's weaknesses," says Tsao. "We build on our hissy fits. Our heated discussions get our asses off the floor and lead us to see things more truthfully." Post-Harvard Tsao worked with Richard Meier and I. M. Pei, and McKown found employment with Ulrich Franzen and Rafael Viñoly until they joined forces in the mid-1980s. Rather than any particular style of design or architecture their firm delivers style with substance and connects the spatial to the spiritual in straightforward modernistic terms, so one day their project board shows their reinvention of a lipstick case while the next day it shows a decade-long conceptualization and construction of an entire city in China.

McKown enjoys beauty for its own sake particularly when there's marked evidence of the maker's hand. "By introducing emotion and intelligence humans have the capacity to create results that rival or even surpass the splendor of nature," he says. "There's a role for the decorative and the whimsical in art and even in architecture providing there's some thought behind it." Tsao continues with a slight digression. "I like fakery," he says. "It's fun. It's a way to offset the hypocrisy of the so-called 'real.'"

Above: The seating and object con-figuration directly opposite the studio's elevator doors led some first-time clients to assume they've mistakenly walked into an antiques warehouse, but nothing here is for sale or rent. The disparity of shapes, materiality, and juxtapositions projected a curious harmony, from the conical wire roof of a nineteenth-century Chinese birdcage to a multi-armed bronze candelabrum, a mercury-glass-topped coffee table, a lychee tree stump, and creamy, cashmerelike sofa upholstery.

Facing page: In an ad hoc library space an early Edison lightbulb perched on an octagonal end table surrounded by a pair of nineteenth-century Chinese Provincial chairs. The books were available to the firm's staff for research or mere browsing and they focused on all aspects of design including fashion. Tsao is particularly inspired by couture and street wear because they involve psychology and cultural mapping.

Overleaf: "All of our belongings engage us in some form of interchange," says McKown. "They're there for the sake of contemplation." A windowsill lineup of photography and art included *Boat Wall* by Phil Smith, *Roman* by Michelle Litvin, *Old Gas Station* by Anders Goldfarb, a char-coal on paper acquired at Larry Collins Fine Art in Provincetown, *Boy* by Jack Pierson, an archival inkjet print from the Rhona Hoffman Gallery also entitled *Boy*, *Production Still* by Gregory Crewdson, and *Mexicana Airbus A320* by Jeffrey Milstein.

DEBORAH EHRLICH & CHRISTOPHER KURTZ

A Charged Spot in the World, a Deluge of Creativity

After Ehrlich bought the 3,600-square-foot house, she opened up a confusing warren of rooms by eliminating dropped ceilings and a number of makeshift interior subdivisions. Post reclamation, her design studio now occupies most of the house's main downstairs room, where a wood cabinet displays a polished assortment of her past and present prototype and production glass wares. The sculpture in the window is by Julie Hedrick; the hanging pendant is part of an ongoing collaboration with E. R. Butler & Co. "Christopher made the Wool Spindle chair," says Ehrlich, "and it influences my work a lot. It looks like nature made it. I see it as a thin piece of wheat balancing against the odds."

The spare beauty and evocative light in their early-eighteenth-century farmhouse passively collaborate in Deborah Ehrlich and Christopher Kurtz's artistic process. "There's a deluge of creativity here—we both feel it," says Ehrlich. "This is a charged little spot in the world."

In the largest room on the ground floor, meticulous drawings covering sheets of paper strewn across Ehrlich's worktable depict the wafer-thin glassware and decanters she designs. Kurtz carves indigenous woods into gravity-defying sculptures and graceful chairs in an airy studio halfway between the house and a cathedral-like Dutch barn where a menagerie of donkeys, geese, cows, and squab once lived. For the most part Kurtz uses manual tools, and Ehrlich is more than content with tracing paper, sharpened pencils, and a ruler in a world where her counterparts are dependent upon CAD technology.

Ehrlich first stumbled upon the abandoned farm after she took a wrong turn one day while house hunting in the Hudson Valley. Its location on a hill overlooking pastures, its timeless brick façade, and its ample porches reminded her of Provence, where she'd once lived. "After I'd walked the property," she recalls, "and spent time in the barn and discovered the waterfall, I knew I could live a sane, grounded life here."

Kurtz moved to the Hudson Valley from rural Kansas City around the same time as Ehrlich to work alongside celebrated sculptor Martin Puryear. "I grew up on the edge of the plains with a feel for the scale of the sky, and here in the Catskills there's a similar sense of openness," he says. Ehrlich was absent when he visited the property with a friend, but he fell in love with her work, and they married six months after their first date. Willa, their daughter, arrived two years later. "It's uncanny. During the five years I assisted Martin I had an hour-long commute to his studio. After I moved in with Deborah I was a long walk away."

Ehrlich was born in New Jersey and after earning a degree in anthropology she studied with sculptor Michael Skop in Kentucky. An extended stay in Europe introduced her to glassblowing, in Copenhagen, and she formed a bond with the Swedish master she commissioned to interpret a set of glassware she designed. "A handworker's state of mind bleeds into anything they make, so even though I consider how a glass feels in the hand and against the lip beyond that I try to transmit joy and silence in my work," she says. "It's why I listen to uplifting

Left: The stone house, dated 1722, sits on 11 bucolic acres of farmland, and its pared-down beauty informs the work of both Ehrlich and Kurtz. "Inspirationally," says Kurtz, "we drink from the same waters."

Facing page: Above Ehrlich's 12-foot-long work-table, clear glass panels, invisibly suspended from a wooden rod, twirl according to atmospheric movement and transitionally reflect the sky or the garden's wisteria or both. Samples of Ehrlich's recent glass vessels sit on rectangular prisms. "Deborah designed their proportions and I replicated them out of lignum vitae, a dense wood with a stonelike feel," says Kurtz. "They migrate around the studio and influence the read of the scale of everything around them. They're her visual and spatial calisthenics." After Ehrlich and Kurtz first met, he shipped her some tumbleweed from New Mexico, and it now occupies one of the window ledges. The chair is the first prototype from Kurtz's Quarter Round collection.

music or read poetry before I sit down to design." The process always appealed to Ehrlich, but she never envisioned herself becoming a designer so she feels as if she fell backward into her current profession. "Glass is magical. It's a mysterious process, an act of faith. Like reaching for a door handle in the dark and finding a structure for the emptiness that's clearly attached to a larger piece of architecture."

When asked, Kurtz slots his work into the margins between art, craft, and design. "I think with my hands," he says. "A chair's sculptural presence, how it relates spatially to its surroundings, is more important to me than its production cost and comfort." Whether his work is functional or not it has precision, poetry, tranquility, and movement. A mobile may have the simplicity of a twirl or the complexity of a spider's web. He only works in wood, and that rigor makes him more innovative while giving integrity to his virtuosic fluency. "My father's a calligrapher and says he could base lifetimes of work on twenty-six letter forms, so I've always equated limitations and freedom of expression."

Sourced from four directions, the studio light has a soft reflectivity as it seeps through the house's original wavy glassed windows and produces a dreamy, starkly romantic quality. "The scale in the windowsill is an object of inspiration for us both," says Kurtz. "It's a constant reminder of formal balance and how important a degree to the left or to the right can be." In musical terms, Ehrlich thinks of the house's atmosphere as more Arvo Pärt than Philip Glass, and Kurtz thinks its austerity and architectural silence renders their work straightforward and exact.

Neither Ehrlich nor Kurtz is particularly materialistic. The house is populated with artwork given by friends, and everything—with the exception of a leaning Masai spear, which to Ehrlich exemplifies perfect design—feels of a piece. "We're not collectors in a traditional sense, maybe because we both create things and enjoy seeing them 'leave home,'" says Kurtz. "An empty studio is one of my favorite things. I like the contrast of not having."

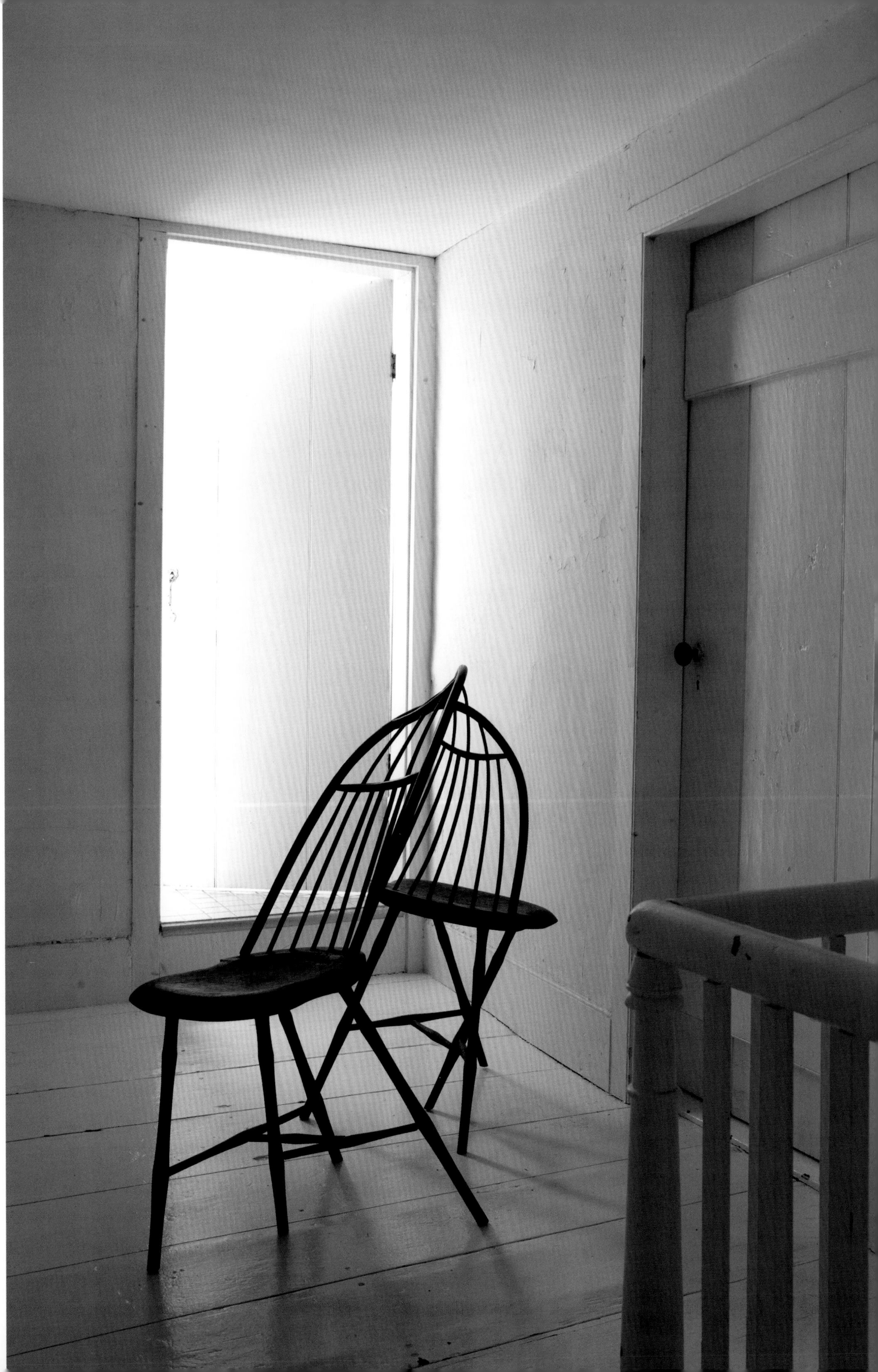

Facing page: White-painted floors amplify the ethereal light on the house's second-floor landing, where Kurtz's sculpture *(A) Typical Windsor Form* lives. "It highlights the anthropomorphic quality of furniture," he says. "It suggests both a graceful dance and a contorted struggle."

Right: The concentric circles of glass in Ehrlich's Double Hurricane lantern intensify and monumentalize a candle's glow and produce multiple reflections. Ehrlich inherited the stack of dinner plates from her grandmother.

Overleaf: Kurtz made most of the furniture that is found in the non-studio portion of the ground floor. Under the window leans one of Ehrlich's favorite paintings, by Diane Szczepaniak, and the triptych hung on the wall is a wedding present from local painter Julie Hedrick, whose late father, Robert Hedrick, made the glass bowl. Ehrlich designed the chaise and Kurtz fabricated it. His daughter Willa inspired the small chairs, and the candlesticks are by Ted Muehling. The glass neon sculpture above the fireplace, by Ned Colclough, was a gift from Kurtz to Ehrlich on their wedding day. "The scale of the windowsills in this house are constant reminders of formal balance," says Kurtz. "They exemplify how important a degree to the left or to the right can be."

In the entry to the house, terrazzo floors
and gold tea-papered walls complement a
1930s lacquer, chrome, and copper console
and an abstract metal wall hanging from
the 1950s. The bulbous bronze sculpture
is by Kathy Webster, a childhood friend
of Johnson's. "The house is four thousand
square feet and it has two parallel wings
connected by a breezeway," says Schwartz,
"so from the air it probably resembles a
pair of binoculars."

ELLEN JOHNSON &
RONNIE SCHWARTZ

If Our Belongings
Had a Gender
It Would be Masculine

When she was a child, Ellen Johnson's father developed such a keen interest in Weimaraners
that he was one of the first people to "import" the aristocratic-looking dogs into Fort Worth,
Texas. Johnson met Ronnie Schwartz in the era before William Wegman's photographs and
Sesame Street popularized the breed. "They are stars these days but thirty-five years ago they
were still relatively rare," says Johnson, "so when I first met Ronnie and learned he'd adopted a
stray I took that as a sign."

To demonstrate how beloved they are, Tom and Stella, the couple's fifth and sixth "Weimies,"
have the choice of fourteen strategically placed beds throughout their New Orleans house but,
furniture purists as they are, Johnson and Schwartz wouldn't dream of permanently sullying
the silhouettes of their couches and armchairs with throws or cushions. "We have pillows
we bring out for guests because some of our chairs and sofas sit deep, but we never leave them
out," says Johnson, a freelance publicist. "And when we watch movies Ronnie generally sits
on his Molino chair and I lay on the floor."

John Lawrence, at one time dean of Tulane's school of architecture, built their 4,000-
square-foot house in 1958. It backs onto a golf course, and its cathedral ceilings dramatize the
silhouettes and patina of Schwartz's stable of furniture and wares from the 1920s through
the 1960s. "That period's compatible with the style of the house," he says. "We didn't want to
live in a time warp." Schwartz, a urologist by profession, began collecting avant-garde 1920s
American Art Deco pieces designed by Paul Frankl when they were still incognito at the
Salvation Army. His father owned thrift shops in East Texas, and summers spent working there
allowed Schwartz to witness firsthand what people cast off. No other factors growing up led
him to believe he would grow into such an avid, determined, and, at times, obsessed collector.

Johnson, an art major, collected postcards and children's books growing up, and now she
has a stash of Bakelite, copper, ivory, rubber, felt, bone, and turquoise jewelry. "I'm tall so I tend
to wear big statement pieces," she says. She sees the pins, bracelets, cuffs, and necklaces she
wears as portable sculptures. "My collecting is more restrained and measured than Ronnie's.
When he latches on to something he has to have it. When we first met he was a solid contender
for one of those television shows that expose hoarders. He had six sofas in his living room,

Left: Acquiring his vintage Mercedes put a crimp in Schwartz's furniture collecting. "I guess I transferred a lot of my furniture passion onto her," he says, "because she has more personality than anything I've owned before." Johnson rescued the six-foot-tall letter E from a marquee atop the Robert E. Lee Theatre in New Orleans when it was demolished in 2009. "I got all ten letters [from the sign] including four Es and a dot," she says, "and I've picked up other Es in more exotic places like Bhutan and Morocco."

all on end, and yet there was nowhere to sit." When they married, substantial storage space was part of the deal and somewhere along the way their interests dovetailed. "Our individual styles are pretty singular and thankfully complementary and they got amplified when we got together," says Johnson. "They blended by osmosis or mutual absorption but we definitely enable each other."

As Texan transplants they both found New Orleans's cultural uniqueness liberating, and it enabled them to develop their own style. Schwartz is self-taught and loves research, and Johnson reckons he could build a guest wing if he stacked up his entire library of auction catalogues. "I love the chase. I get fixated," he says. "Then once I've come in for the kill and it's mine I move on to the next. That's not to say that the things I own aren't characters in my life." Johnson describes their mutual decorating style as potluck with a flexible color scheme that accommodates the original upholstery of anything they happen to acquire, although the master bedroom is the exception with its coordinated neutrals that are quiet and soft. "That and our guest bedroom feel quite feminine but if our house and its contents had a gender," says Johnson, "it would be masculine."

In recent years Schwartz ventured outside his decades-long comfort zone when he purchased his first vintage car, a 1957 Mercedes-Benz 300 SL roadster. Johnson refers to it as the "other woman" and calls it "Luscious" because it's often Schwartz's primary focus. "She's younger than me and she's drop-dead gorgeous," says Johnson, "and she provides the outlet for our adventure and travel bug when she takes us to MB 300 SL annual conventions at primo destinations across the country." Growing up Johnson was often the designated driver, but Schwartz won't allow her behind the steering wheel, which often qualifies as a bone of contention. "I don't mean it to be sexist," says Schwartz. "It's just that the car has a greater significance than any piece of furniture I've ever owned. It's as if it has a life of its own because it has a lot of characteristics of a social animal. It's caused me to reevaluate how I look at chairs."

Clockwise from top left: An arrangement of objects on top of a dresser includes a turquoise necklace formerly owned by the minimalist artist Dan Flavin; one half of a vintage doll mold; a crawfish and a praying mantis embedded in Lucite; a wooden purse by Shinichi Miyazaki; a Marc Brasz photograph Schwartz scored after he recognized the smoker as the same subject of a large Brasz painting he owned; and a mixed-media "fetish egg" conceptualized by New Orleans artist Elizabeth Shannon.

At the other end of the entrance hall, an African wooden bowl sits on a Walter Von Nessen table from the 1920s and holds Johnson's twenty-year-old collection of wishbones. The mixed-media fabric, thread, and acrylic-paint portrait is from a series Gina Phillips created with Fats Waller as her muse. The wooden ladle is from Mali, and the pair of 1930s bronze boxers hail from the Hagenauer workshop.

In the study the wood paneling and ceiling fixture are original to the house. The scale of the Bakelite drawer pulls on the French 1930s desk is reminiscent of Johnson's jewelry, and the chair is classic 1950s Thonet. Gae Aulenti's iconic La Ruspa lamp from 1958 faces a 1940s red metal car and a George Nelson clock from the 1950s. The digital panel photo of Johnson and Schwartz is by Lew Thomas, and the rectangular oil on canvas by Steve Wheeler dates back to 1946. Most of their Weimaraners, including Tom and Stella, were adopted.

Left: Paul T. Frankl designed the cork and mahogany dining table and set of six upholstered chairs in the 1940s, and Schwartz refers to *Form and Reform*, the designer's 1930s handbook, as his bible. Robert Sonneman's aluminum chandelier is from the 1960s; the cabinet is attributed to Edward Wormley; and a WPA artist, Kenneth Bradley Loomis, painted the oil on canvas in the mid-1930s. Ceramics range from Russel Wright, on the table, to Mancioli, on the cabinet. The E is from a large sculpture by Steve Rucker and its partner, R, is in storage.

Right: Johnson feels the guest bedroom has a visual sweetness. The wood and rattan George Nelson bed and the Greta Magnusson-Grossman standing lamp are both from the 1950s as are the wall sconces that are original to the house. Lesley Dill's *Copper Poem Suit* pays homage to Emily Dickinson, and Angel Delgado created *Nine Handkerchiefs* in a Cuban prison.

Facing page: In the living room the Carlo Molino armchair is a reproduction; the sofa is a 1929 Paul T. Frankl design; the laminated birch, lead, and glass table dates from the 1930s; and the slatted bench is 1950s George Nelson. On the mantle, the wood head is probably seventy years old; the two ceramic musicians came from a local vintage store; *The Red Chair* is a portrait of Schwartz by Georganne Deen; and the aluminum E started Johnson off on her alphabetical quest. The pair of nineteenth-century ventriloquist dummies came from auction, and the large canvas, entitled *The Egg Man*, is, by far, Schwartz's favorite painting. "I haven't been able to attribute it, which is a shame," he says, "but its scale, demarcation lines, color, and hard edges epitomize everything I'm drawn to in art."

44

In the entry hall a nineteenth-century Chinese elm altar table sits centrally in front of a wall of randomly hung nineteenth-century oil portraits. De Vera originally thought about installing a chandelier here but instead he painstakingly created a functional melted wax sculpture. "All of our curiosities, knowledge, likes, and dislikes are unique," he says. "In my case, I communicate my personality and my life through the things I make and present, so by looking at them you see who I am."

FEDERICO DE VERA

The Unconventional and Curious Lingering in the Mind's Eye

A born storyteller, Federico de Vera builds visual narratives with statuary, artifacts, artwork, and furniture and whatever else he's drawn to. No matter whether the object is primitive, stylized, or macabre, his ability to uncover harmony in the disparate is second nature, as is his desire to regard the precious and the found as equals. To him a ruby is akin to a bent key so long as they both meet his definition of beauty. By not restricting his taste to one genre or aesthetic, his arrangements celebrate the cross-pollination and marriage of them all. The en masse displays throughout his upstate New York house— an entire wall of oil portraits, a tablescape of wax-laden candlesticks, a dozen mismatched chairs—blend the unconventional with the curious and linger in the mind's eye. "I equate sensory overload with a good novel that you can't put down," he says. "Where you savor every sentence because you don't want it to end."

By contrast, the inventory of marble busts, contemporary glassware, weathered relics, Georgian jewelry, wood milagros, ivory netsukes, taxidermy, porcelain goblets, and insect samplers in his two eponymous Manhattan stores is more tightly edited. He carefully configures it in shrinelike vitrines until each one stands as a concise statement about democratic beauty. "I love research so I consider the history of every object I buy, but my first instinct is to focus on its architecture, luster, and inherent appeal," he says. "Its provenance, association with a celebrity, or affiliation with a particular design movement isn't enough to seduce me." He creates subtexts for his tableaux but keeps them to himself because he feels they're irrelevant to the process of appreciation. "The composition has to speak for itself," he says. "It's why I'd never use one of those guided museum tapes where the curator talks you through an exhibit. That strikes me as a spoilt experience waiting to happen."

De Vera commutes to his house every weekend in every season and enjoys napping in most of its rooms. Thanks to his landscape design, the converted 1875 train station looks as if it landed in the middle of a field. The large boulders, beds of stones, boxwood hedges, and rows of sleepy willow shrubs he placed and planted have the rigor of a Japanese garden and the randomness of a countryside stroll. Sky views stretch off into the distance oblivious to electrical power lines and neighbors so the setting feels centuries old. "If you scan all the rooms you learn a lot about me because all this stuff's essentially my diary from way, way back," he says. "I still have the first etching I ever bought in auction. I have some rocks I've owned forever, as well as some rusty tools and books. An ex is fond of one of my paintings and regularly asks me if he can have it, and I always

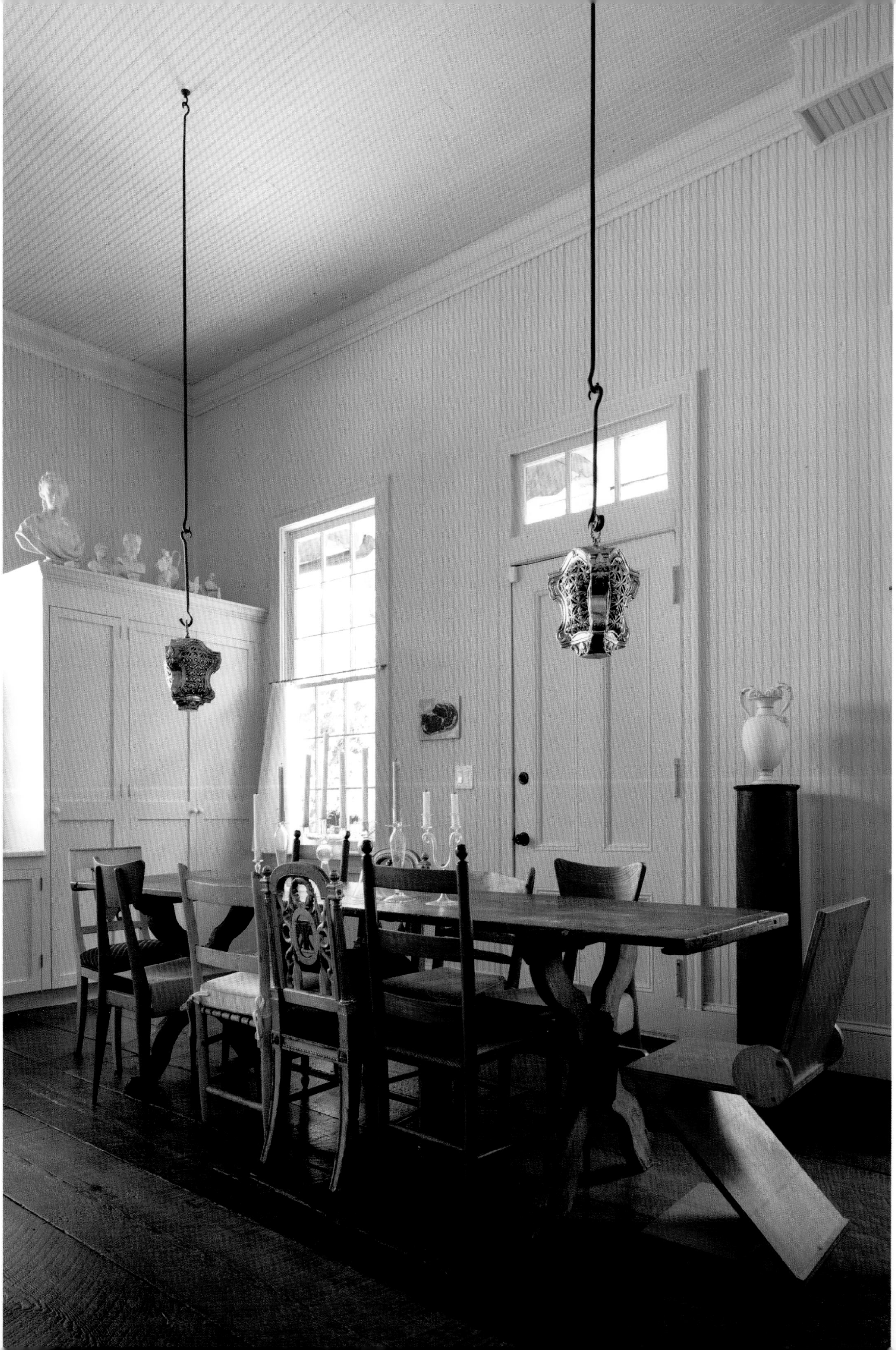

Facing page: In De Vera's hands, ten mismatched chairs—some pairs, some loners, rustic, gilt, geometric—placed around a French trestle table feel like a cohesive dining set. A pair of hanging silver lanterns he purchased in Peru resemble chunky costume jewelry and are overseen by several bisque and porcelain busts. In a Baroque meets minimalism gesture, the setup shares one half of a room with a pristine stainless steel and Carrera marble kitchen.

Left: A lineup of nude sculptures on a French school library table in the main living room reminds De Vera of Jean Prouvé. "I used to define beauty as form meeting function," he says, "but nowadays I believe that the sole purpose of certain things is to simply radiate beauty."

say, 'Nope. That comes with me!'" Besides his feisty Chihuahua, Diego, his most treasured possession is a photograph of his mother taken during the 1950s, when she was in her twenties. It hangs on the inside of his bedroom door where he can view it in private. "She hates that image because she's sweeping the floor and feels as if she looks like a maid, but to me it's as emotionally stirring and haunting as Picasso's *Woman Ironing.*" De Vera's family still lives in the Philippines, where he was born, and as one of ten children in the family he remembers picking up pieces of weathered driftwood and pitted stones on his regular beach jaunts. "I'd place them around my bedroom, and my mother routinely gathered them up and threw them out," he recalls, "but that didn't stop me. Finally, she gave up! The hunter-gatherer instinct is still in me as is the need to hold, feel, and touch everything I acquire, which is why I never buy online."

From the age of six he played piano and settled on creative writing as a means of expression but he never envisioned himself in one particular career or another. "My older sister, who's now a successful businesswoman, once told me to never pursue a profession purely for money. She said, 'choose something you enjoy and the money will come of its own accord,' and I never forgot her advice. I guess following my heart and communicating my visual instincts worked out for me."

He remembers periods of having little money, when the high sticker price of an object he coveted amounted to a huge investment. "I still associate desire with sacrifice and I still place a greater value on something I couldn't easily afford," he says. "Maybe that's why I don't offer seasonal sales in my stores. In many ways, money can be destructive. When people have tons of disposable cash their objects are also often disposable." A large chunk of de Vera's clientele belongs to the tastemaker set, but nevertheless he steers clear of purchasing anything trendy. "I also run in the opposite direction of fake—things or people," he says. "Consequently all of my friends are genuine and generous. They have good hearts and they're also spontaneous and funny. When I look back at people I admire in the design and art worlds—Carlo Scarpa, Josef Hoffmann, Gustav Mahler—I imagine hitting it off with them really well."

The unique, rare, unscathed pieces he acquires generally feed his businesses, while the broken and the leftover seem to end up in his New York apartment or his house. "When an object is old and it's still in good condition, decades or centuries of careful handling get distilled into a palpable kind of energy," he says. "Even though I'm materially attached I don't really feel as if I actually possess anything. I feel like a guardian, a person who's passing through a tiny portion of an object's lifespan. At the same time I can't stand to think about all my belongings ending up in a garage sale after I die. That thought is an absolute nightmare."

Right: On one wall of the dining room a wall-mounted taxidermy pheasant hangs alongside a functioning nineteenth-century Norwegian cast-iron stove.

Below: De Vera doesn't treat anything he owns in a precious way, so his cheeky Chihuahua has free rein to roam on all the furniture, including a Venetian armchair that's upholstered with antique Rubelli fabric. He found the pouffe-like "tomato" chair in Prague and reckons it was formerly part of a stage set. A piece of glass functions as a table with an antique Indian stone capital as its base, and the bronze Marcus Aurelius bust dates from the nineteenth century.

Facing page: In a second-floor sitting area De Vera didn't want Darren Waterston's painting *Agony In the Garden* to float on a white wall, so he backed it with a Mughal silk and gold-thread bedspread. On a simple Jacobean table he arranged Venetian glass, German iron candlesticks, Baroque architectural elements, and a Cire Trudon candle that references a Jean-Antoine Houdon bust.

Overleaf: A salon-style arrangement of paintings, prints, drawings, and photography fills the living room's entrance and includes works by Michael Huey, Richard Barnes, Jean Arp, Danny Keith, Nicolas de Staël, Darren Waterston, Pablo Picasso, Alberto Giacometti, Henry Moore, Agelio Batle, Brigitte Lacombe, J. John Priola, Nicholas Nixon, František Drtikol, and Alphonse Legros. "These walls represent twenty-five years of collecting," says De Vera. "I trade objects on a daily basis but my art is different. I'm reluctant to part with any of it."

Facing page: A regiment of lingams De Vera shipped in from Rajasthan acts as a tactical doorstop, preventing guests from walking directly into the dining area.

Right: A nineteenth-century marble statue of orator Aeschines is stationed in front of a tall boxwood hedge that conceals his property from the old railroad that now functions as a walking trail.

Below: The former passenger and freight station still has its original ticket booth. De Vera restored the building's entire structure but added nothing architecturally. "I made it look as if it's always been here," he says. Two iron urns function as gas fire pits, and the 13-foot-long teak bench affords De Vera his favorite view of the property.

Overleaf: A long nineteenth-century Italian daybed echoes the living room's strict architectural symmetry, while the rest of the furniture comes in every conceivable shape, size, and texture. Sliding barn doors pocket into glass-fronted cabinets where De Vera stores design books and a multitude of precisely arranged artifacts.

In the living room a George III mahogany secretary displays locally found seashells. The 1950s tropical wallpaper originally hung in the Boom Boom Room in Miami Beach's legendary Fontainebleau Hotel, and Meyer designed the seahorse rug with his brother, Doug.

GENE MEYER & FRANK DE BIASI

Casualness and Beigeness Are OK, but What Then?

"When it comes to color, my parents were fearless," says Gene Meyer, recalling the decor of his elegantly modern childhood home in Louisville, Kentucky. "There was a lot of white to match the mid-century and Swedish modern furniture but it always had its zany counterpart. At one point our den had tartan wool carpeting and chromium yellow corduroy upholstery. And then there was my father dressed in one of his crazy Lilly Pulitzer golf outfits. Back then, in the context of the psychedelic 1960s, our home didn't register as particularly 'out there.'" Needless to say, Meyer's mother didn't seriously consider her decorator's suggestion to tone things down with a few charcoal gray accents. Like Meyer, she felt "life has a perfect spot for every shade you like," so she applauded her husband when he proposed painting the house's double entry doors electric pink.

"I clearly inherited their daring," says Meyer, "and I clearly come from a family of restless decorators." In one of his mother's many schemes, his teenage bedroom ended up with a visually tight composition of Plexiglas lamps and striped wallpaper. "I was a hippie at the time and I freaked because it was too 'done,' so I wallpapered everything, even the ceiling, with large Peter Max posters. It was anything but restful." The decoupage transitioned into a coordinated brown and orange theme once Meyer discovered Billy Baldwin, and his current definition of heaven involves chartreuse, coral, and turquoise.

He spent a year at the Louisville School of Art and went on to attend Parsons in New York, where his designs won several awards. He defines his first job assisting fashion designer Geoffrey Beene as "eleven years at couturier school," and he left in 1989 to launch his own clothing label. Resembling a hip version of Matisse's paper cutouts, his silk, color-blocked men's ties from the early 1990s still look current and are still coveted. His primary-to-pastel ratio is thought to have perfect pitch, and whenever it comes time to establish the colorways for the lines of furniture, textiles, and carpets he currently creates with his younger brother Doug, he feels as if he's about to go on holiday.

Meyer lives with Frank de Biasi, his partner of eighteen years, who grew up in the suburbs of Richmond, Virginia, where his schooling felt like an immersion course in Civil War history. Extracurricular study exposed him to periods and regions beyond the Anglo-loving

Left: The main house on Meyer and de Biasi's Biscayne Bay property connects to a cottage through a striped patio breezeway, and the pattern sets guests up for a riotously decorated sitting room. In turn, the painted, exposed ceiling joists set the precedent for the vertical banding on the walls. Meyer's father created the largest of four drawings in the 1950s, and one of Meyer's oversize printed cotton scarves moonlights as a curtain.

Facing page: The 1930s/1940s bamboo mirror and cabinet are local finds. "One of the intentions behind the scheme here is to perceptibly heighten the room," says Meyer. "All the greens set up a kind of vibration. I'm always seeking out some kind of tension when I match colors. When things are slightly 'off' I know I've hit the right palette."

south, and once he realized he was a Francophile at heart he enrolled at the Sorbonne. A subsequent six-year stint as an appraiser at Christie's in New York gave him entrée into a plethora of spectacular estates and led to twelve years as Peter Marino's director of interiors. He started his own firm in 2006. His clients tend to define livability in safe, neutral terms, so he finds his collaborations with Meyer liberating. "We're a team and we work well together. Gene's bold, he's a free spirit, while I take the macro approach," says de Biasi. "We both respect what we grew up with but our mutual thirst is for something different."

The Manhattan loft they share has tall ceilings, an extensive design library, and tons of edgy art; their Parisian apartment, located in a late-eighteenth-century building in the 6th arrondissement, has marble floors, distressed walls, and *faux bois* finishes. Their 1941 Bahamian-style cottage in Miami is a veritable kaleidoscope of chintz, charm, and Chinoiserie with nods to Morocco and Mustique. A painterly folly, its hand-applied finishes are as whimsical as they are complex. Stripes, serrated lines, and star and diamond patterns transform incidental passageways and nondescript corners into animated focal points. Plaster sea horses cavort across a chimney breast; hand-painted seashells stud a threshold arch. Inspired by porch details in a house designed by Oliver Messel, de Biasi trimmed a bookcase with scalloped friezes; Meyer, meanwhile, auditioned more than fifty colors before he hit on a perfect compatibility in the sitting room's striped walls. "For some reason," says Meyer, "most of our neighbors painted their interiors in washed-out Santa Fe colors, which strikes us as pretty strange."

The Bonnet House, a historic 1920s Fort Lauderdale estate, motivated Meyer and de Biasi to layer, sequence, and saturate all their treatments, particularly in the dining room, where pelmets, panels, chair rails, and skirting boards practically share a painter's wand. Far from experiencing a bout of color deprivation, Meyer finds it relatively easy to relax in nonvibrant spaces. "When it's temporary I find it refreshing because there's no distraction. In the hand of a brilliant colorist beige is surely comfortable," he says, "but I couldn't live without the joy, formality, and theatricality of color. I mean, casualness and beigeness are OK, but then what?"

Above: "Pink is the most flattering color, especially at night," says Meyer. "And when it's mixed with candlelight there's nothing more flattering—everyone's complexion glows." In the main house's living room, 1940s plaster casts of seahorses cavort on the chimney breast. The low table, designed by Karl Springer, is a thrift shop find, the 1950s curtain and slipcover chintz came from a Paris flea market, and the ceramic bird sculpture is by Peter Schlesinger.

Right: The foyer doubles as an overflow library. "We wanted the walls to have a matte distemper, as if they were outside," says de Biasi. Meyer spent several weeks collecting, placing, gluing, and then painting all the shells, and he hand carried the tiger rug back from Nepal.

Facing page: "The red and chartreuse incarnation of this room was short-lived," says de Biasi. "The color combination didn't feel very tropical so it wasn't very conducive to dining. We've never gotten around to painting the ceiling, and the scallop on the crown is another simple nod to Oliver Messel, except we went a little further and customized it with the starfish."

GEORGE LINDEMANN

Interacting with
Beauty May Scuff but
It's Life Enhancing

Lindemann asked Austin Harrelson to supervise a renovation of the house, and the interior designer eliminated a few walls to enhance its flow. Harrelson also had carte blanche to rifle through Lindemann's extensive, well-catalogued archive and bring whatever he wanted out of storage. In the dining area a jewel-like Robert Goossens chandelier hangs above a 1970s Wendell Castle table and chairs set in front of a blurred target painting by Ugo Rondinone. "Wendell's stuff has increased in value since I first bought it," says Lindemann, "and I admit it, that fact enhances the experience of sitting."

"It started off with one cactus and they kept on multiplying," says George Lindemann, explaining how his first encounter with collecting wasn't exactly planned. "I took care of them for well over a decade, which is a long time when you're a kid." Cut to today, when the country's top auctioneers and dealers consider Lindemann to be one of Miami's most impassioned experts on contemporary sculpture, paintings, and furnishings. "It's hard to track how my taste evolved from there to here or to predict where it will lead because it changes as I age and as I accumulate more experiences, so in that sense it's random. It mirrors wherever I am in my life."

Lindemann grew up on the east side of Manhattan and at an age when his schoolmates were likely trading baseball cards, he saved every ticket he ever bought to ride the Fifth Avenue bus as it made its way across 70th Street. "There was a different color each month," he remembers, "and I still have every pass issued to me from the third through the twelfth grade stacked neatly with rubber bands and filed inside a shoe box."

Not everything in the world of ephemera lasts forever, and Lindemann had a rude awakening when he first moved to Miami and showed museum owner Micky Wolfson Jr. a large set of American nineteenth-century plein air watercolors created by explorers documenting the American expansion into the west. "I was pretty naïve, and Micky pointed out the obvious—that the Floridian climate would ruin the paper," he says. From that point on the chief criteria for anything he set his eye on was its capacity to withstand Miami's light, heat, and humidity. "Now whenever I fall in love with something, if it's not compatible with the weather I have to let it go."

As president of the Bass Museum, Lindemann focuses on the ever-shifting intersection of art, design, and fashion in contemporary culture and traces the dividing line between the three disciplines as it gradually fades into obscurity. "Fashion by its very nature cycles according to trends, but I never succumb to 'what's in and what's out' when I buy," he says. "The appeal of any object is whether it resonates for me personally, whether it commemorates an event or a life transition, or whether the maker's grappled with or resolved a particular idea or theory I find intriguing. I've owned some of my possessions for more than three decades and they still make me happy and I find that reassuring on so many levels."

Left: In the master bedroom a table lamp by Robert Goossens rests on one of a pair of Mattia Bonetti commodes. "There are supposed to be three," says Lindemann, "but I put one in storage because it didn't fit into this corner. I'm not sure what Mattia would think, but I call it 'owner's *liberté*.'"

Facing page: "It's a lifer," says Lindemann of his aluminum-framed Jean-Michel Othoniel bed. Adorned with garlands of blue and red Murano glass orbs, it sits on a Mattia Bonetti rug alongside a bronze elephant side table designed by Claude and François-Xavier Lalanne.

Overleaf: In the spacious living room Marc Newson's biomorphic Orgone table sits low on a Mattia Bonetti rug. Simulating a sinuous tangle of branches, Claude and François-Xavier Lalanne's bronze and copper Lustre chandelier hovers over Damien Hirst's wall-mounted cabinet, entitled *Fear*, from his Entomology series. The gold coffee table and chairs set is by Wendell Castle, and the untitled piece on the wall is by Anselm Reyle. "I'm less interested in conceptual pieces of design," says Lindemann. "I gravitate toward surfaces where there's evidence of the maker's hand."

The 1950s bungalow he shares with his wife and children sits in an amiable mani-cured neighborhood on La Gorce, an island off Miami whose old world elegance seems a million miles away from nearby South Beach and its pulsating nightlife. Unlike most of the island's real estate, Lindemann's house has no direct view of the bay, but no matter. It's a tem-porary stopgap while he builds a house a short distance away in Sunset Islands.

His four children know they can't touch the art and that small-scale objects don't respond well to tiny fingers, but the furniture is definitely not off limits. The celebrated crafts-man Wendell Castle designed the family's breakfast and dining tables, and the kids normally sit on a Napoleon campaign chair when they put their shoes on to go to school, and book bags invariably end up on one of a pair of bronze Lalanne elephant tables. "They're all museum-quality pieces," he says, "but on a daily basis we're pretty oblivious to that. I recently initiated one of my daughters by giving her a massive pink and gold egg created by the Japanese cerami-cist Takuro Kuwata. She loved it because pink is her favorite color." In Lindemann's mind designers actively want people to interact with their furniture. "Spilt milk is easy to wipe away and all the legs of our chairs have scuffs but that's why restoration exists. It's life enhancing to interact with beautiful things."

A behavior-altering conversation a few years ago with Castle brought on Lindemann's current laissez-faire. "I showed him a pair of Student chairs he designed more than fifty years ago out of solid walnut and expressed how nervous I was about using them," he says. "With that he climbed on one of the cantilevers to demonstrate its durability and bounced up and down a couple of times. After that my caution evaporated."

The Eames chair is one of a set of two Yanagihara found abandoned—with their original stickers still on their undercarriage—on the street in the West Village. The picture is from Tomoko Sawada's ID400 four-part series, with each composed of one hundred photo-booth images of the photographer in different guises. The cushion is from one of her favorite interiors stores, Mustapha Blaoui, in Marrakech.

HANYA YANAGIHARA

In a Spare, Neutral Space I'd Feel Permanently Adrift

On any given day Hanya Yanagihara's approaching itinerary is likely to resemble a major airline's international departures board. A travel editor and novelist, her first book, *The People in the Trees*, focuses on a fictional lost tribe, while her witty, evocative blog documents her real global adventures. One entry shows the loosely packed bag she lived out of on a fifty-one-day trip through Asia. But her Manhattan loft shows no such minimalist ingenuity.

"I find myself in anonymous airports and generic hotel rooms for extended periods of time, so my living space needs to be highly personal and to me that spells abundance. I'm constantly subjugated to other people's tastes so if my home was neutral and spare I'd feel permanently adrift in the world," she says. "As I'm not doing this for anyone else I can indulge in all of my aesthetic fantasies from the frivolous to the oddly masculine. The most interesting homes have some fundamental conflict at their core and without a doubt I prefer bad taste to no taste at all. I'll take Pee Wee's Playhouse over a Westin Hotel room any day."

A fourth-generation Japanese-American, Yanagihara grew up in Hawaii, Los Angeles, East Texas, and Baltimore before she settled in New York. Her parents, who are both accomplished craftspeople, compensated for all the relocations by creating characterful living spaces and passed their respect for art, workmanship, and heritage on to their daughter. "I always knew I would become a collector, like them," she says, "but it wasn't until my early twenties when I realized it was a part of my DNA and as necessary to me as eating. Now I see it as a lovely way for us all to maintain a dialogue."

After she bought her 1,200-square-foot loft she commissioned architect Steve Blatz to resolve its oppressively funky layout, and he proposed housing her extensive library in a monolithic shelving system. She gave away 2,000 volumes, and her current tightly edited inventory of 7,500 novels, art books, and first editions is methodically alphabetized according to authors' surnames. "When people arrange their books by color it tells me they are not serious readers," she says. "Books aren't meant to be purely decorative."

By cleaving the loft in two the freestanding bookcase separates the personal and private areas, promotes ventilation, and forces a circulation of traffic. It also frees up enough wall space for a salon-style arrangement of around 250 framed photographs that include early works by Araki and obscure pieces by Naoki Ishikawa. "I want guests to be assaulted by the art as soon as

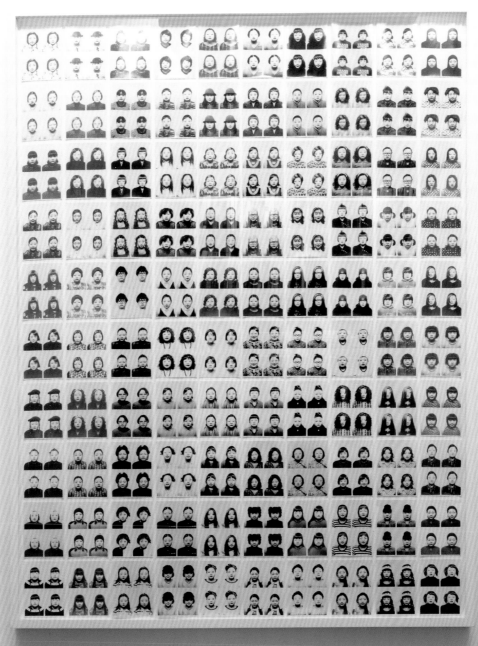

In the loft's blue hallway Yanagihara hung rows of photographs taken by Hiroh Kikai, Liu Zheng, and Tseng Kwong Chi, a contemporary of Keith Haring's. "I only frame large, fragile work, and I never display personal pictures," she says. "My father always thought that was tacky and I agree with him. In fact, I never even take personal pictures." The chair is a 1790 Philadelphia Chippendale with an early-nineteenth-century silk upholstered seat. "Throughout my childhood," she remembers, "it was like another family member with a status somewhere between beloved pet and child. I sat on it once a year for a portrait and occasionally the cat took up residence."

they walk in," she says. The installers took ten hours to map and two hours to hang the collection according to Yanagihara's plan for a lively mix of colors, sizes, genres, mediums, and textures. To preserve artwork she keeps window shades drawn so the space is visually vibrant and in a perpetual twilight state. "My mother told me she was glad I'd found a place to die in and that startled me at first until I had the epiphany that tombs traditionally contained all the accoutrements a soul needed to happily transition into the hereafter. Since then I've been at peace with the concept."

She has slept on her 1800s American colonial bed since she was eight. Back then she was never allowed to sit on it during the day and at night she had to lie perfectly still because tossing and turning might tear its fragile rope frame. "I never saw it as a place of rest," she says. "I saw it as an uncooperative piece of furniture and every time I slept on it I had the distinct feeling it was doing me a huge favor." She reluctantly accepted it as a gift from her parents, but now with a new custom box spring and mattress it provides one of the best sleeping experiences she's ever had. "Just as important," she says, "the bed's presence proves that a good piece of furniture, no matter its provenance, can live anywhere, with any kind of design whether it's modern Danish with Colonial American, eighteenth-century Korean, or contemporary Italian."

While she didn't think twice about hiring an architect, consulting an interior decorator was never in the cards. "It's not in my nature to cede my entire visual personality to another person," she says. "If our clothes express who we are to the outside world then our interiors express our inner lives: who and what we represent to ourselves. When I walk into a home I derive comfort from knowing there's a real live beating heart behind its decor. In here I palpably feel the pride and love the artists and artisans invested in their work and I hope that comes across."

In Yanagihara's bedroom, her mother's intricate hand-stitching is evident in the quilt's traditional, appliquéd pattern of crowns and kahilis. The top painting above the bed is by Naoto Kawahara and the one below is by Yoriko Kita. The Mexican wrestler head on the sill is from Bungalow 8 in Mumbai, another of her favorite retail haunts. On the desk the skull sculpture is by Ken Kagami; Yanagihara has owned the two Navajo dolls since she was seven; she bought the pair of cloth dolls at the night market in Luang Prabang, Laos; the deformed Noh mask is by Motohiko Odani; and the framed photograph, entitled *Charles*, is by Alec Soth.

The three pictures in the column between the windows are by Tomoko Sawada from her Omiai series. The photo on the top corner is one half of Sze Tsung Leong's diptych *Causeway Bay*, which bookends the entire wall. Each of the two images measures 72 by 87 inches unframed, and because they wouldn't fit in the elevator or stairwell they were craned into the building. More wall space would allow her to hang some of the ikats she acquired abroad as well as some of her mother's beloved hand-sewn quilts.

Above: The limited-edition pink Wegner chairs commemorate breast cancer awareness. Yanagihara commissioned their seat cushions from textiles she'd picked up at markets in Istanbul and Kyoto. As well as the oversize Sze Tsung Leong photograph there are works by Loretta Lux, Simen Johan, and Andrea Modica.

Overleaf: Architect Steve Blatz ingeniously created the bookcase by metal plating and spray-painting an inexpensive prefab unit; at its center hangs Hiroshi Sugimoto's *Bass Strait.* "I always coveted his work and I bought this piece while I was unemployed and desperately freelancing," says Yanagihara. "I contacted his Tokyo gallery, Koyanagi, which graciously gave me a nice discount and then let me pay the piece off very, very slowly over the course of two years."

A framed silk square hangs on the Monticello-yellow dining room wall of Llewellyn's house in Kingston, New York. "We refer to it as the 'drunken scarf,'" he says, "because I bought it as a gift for my grandmother after I'd spent my sixteenth birthday drinking champagne at the Lido in Paris. It was twisted into swirls, so I never saw its design of racy, nude ladies until I returned home and handed it to her. Subsequently it became one of her favorite accessories." A terra-cotta bust sits alongside a nineteenth-century carved wood conch on an eighteenth-century Boston bow-fronted chest. The chair is English Chippendale and the etched crystal urn is Italian.

HAYNES LLEWELLYN

Sometimes I Feel I'm on the Border of a Hoarder Disorder

"In my family home in Alabama I had variations and incarnations of the same furnishings and knickknacks I have around me now, so I guess my taste is inherited," says Haynes Llewellyn. "Passing things along generationally—idiosyncratic traditions, heirlooms, recipes—is a characteristically Southern phenomenon. It's how the region retains its identity." An interior designer and active preservationist in the upstate New York region where he owns an 1840s Greek Revival–style house, Llewellyn sums up his mother's taste, and arguably his own, as "composed decoration. *The Philadelphia Story* minus the swank."

"Gracious" is the word he ascribes to the behavior and lifestyle of his childhood neighbors in Georgia. "They all owned beautifully appointed nineteenth-century houses, manicured yards bordered by mature trees, and exquisite flower beds, and they frequently sold antiques out of their living rooms," he remembers. Swag purchased on weekly Llewellyn family outings to craft fairs, junk shops, and flea markets served to bolster existing collections of pewter, blue china, Chippendale chairs, and miniature boxes.

As a toddler, spurred on by his grandfather's hobbies of whittling decoys, reproducing eighteenth-century furniture, and repairing mantel clocks, Llewellyn occasionally leafed through an interior design magazine. "The family subscribed to every one that ever was," he remembers, "but I came into my own once I discovered the *World of Interiors* when I was in college."

Some mothers sharpen their children's wits by asking them to conjugate verbs or recite multiplication tables, but Llewellyn was routinely quizzed about the contents and layouts of houses the family visited. "My mother expected nothing less than total recall," he says, "which is why my sense of color is still so acute."

Soon after he left college he bought the contents of a neighbor's estate sale, and in retrospect that considerable haul—a set of fiddleback chairs, several gilt and Eastlake wooden frames with mother-of-pearl inlays, and flow blue and Chinese export bowls and plates—established him as a full-fledged collector. "At that moment in time I realized how comfortable it felt to have things around me I deeply cared about, and that's still the case. I recently came across an 1820s English barometer with a walnut case identical to one owned by an old friend, so I bought it knowing it would bring fond memories of her. Being on a limited budget limits my consumption, but I'm always wary of turning into a magpie. I imagine things

Left: In one of the ground-floor sitting rooms a rare Herend statue sits on a demi-lune table in front of shelves displaying nineteenth-century Wedgwood, vintage Italian porcelain by Mottahedeh, and Chinese porcelain bowls from the eighteenth century. "Tradition is comfortingly familiar," says Llewellyn. "It anchors you to your roots. I don't think I could ever live in a brand-new house or apartment."

Facing page: Llewellyn bought the large canvas at the Georgetown Flea Market; its painter is unknown. An English George III card table supports a bust by Canadian artist Annemarie Slipper and a nineteenth-century bronze oil lamp. The Chippendale chair is eighteenth century, its seat cover is vintage hand-blocked Schumacher fabric, and the wall is a Nancy Lancaster yellow. "I've always liked strong colors—nothing washed out or pastel," says Llewellyn. "In fact the bolder, the better."

passing through my life, but that's far from the reality. Sometimes I feel as if I'm on the border of a hoarder disorder."

Llewellyn's partner, Gary Swenson, a legal technology consultant, is anything but a collector. "My mother was a prolific needlepoint artist, but beyond that I never paid a mind to all of this before I met Haynes. Now I feel as if I could host the *Antiques Roadshow*," he says. "Eighteenth-century American is considered to be the Holy Grail around here, but I prefer the English pieces."

Llewellyn isn't 100 percent faithful to his ancestral aesthetic. He banned damask and brocade because he finds them fussy, and he doesn't subscribe to the formality of preserving certain rooms for "company." His three Scottie dogs, Heather, Mac, and Frazier, are free to stretch out on the upholstery, and each room, even the kitchen, has an assigned reading nook. "I never design bedrooms per se. I design gathering spaces that happen to have beds in them," he says. "That's why our ten-room house only accommodates one guest."

A born host, Llewellyn loves to entertain, and consequently he's familiar with all the tricks and pitfalls of throwing a cocktail party for a hundred at the drop of a hat. "When you routinely entertain, breakages are par for the course and occasionally things get damaged. Furniture's repairable but porcelain and glassware is something else," he says. "Once a crystal goblet or a plate breaks it's pretty tragic. In extreme cases when it involves something I'm particularly fond of it almost feels like a death in the family."

In many ways the house's decor duplicates Llewellyn's wardrobe. It's a perfect backdrop for his Brooks Brothers jackets, Gucci loafers, Gianfranco Ferre ties, and Paul Smith shirts with French cuffs, not to mention the Hermès pocket squares he wears as a way of remembering his grandmother. His mother has a healthy assortment of teapots and for a while, as an affectionate gesture, he collected cups and saucers. "Then one day I realized they were giving me the heebie-jeebies so I unloaded them," he says. "I don't want anything around me that gets me agitated. My tradition is to take the past by the hand and ever so gently bring it into the present day."

Right: A nineteenth-century leather and gilt fireplace screen sets off a Casa Stradivari chair. Llewellyn often stacks books on his dining table or he randomly piles them around the sitting room, where they double as ad hoc drinks tables. "I don't just browse through coffee table books," he says. "I'm one of the rare breed who actually reads them cover to cover!"

Below: In a corner of the ground floor's back living room, an eclectic mix of furnishings includes an eighteenth-century English Chippendale chair, pairs of porcelain Foo Dogs and Delft temple jars, a nineteenth-century Japanese figure, a plaster column, a 1910 French chest, an eighteenth-century bull's-eye mirror, and drawings by Antonio Barone.

Facing page: The sitting room to the right of the house's entrance contains a nineteenth-century Chinese Chippendale sofa uphol-stered in Ralph Lauren fabric, an eighteenth-century American tea table, a Chippendale stool from the 1800s, a nineteenth-century Chinoiserie game box with bronze feet, and a nineteenth-century French bronze statue of Mercury. The painting was a housewarming gift from Llewellyn's mother. "It reminds us of Josephine Baker," he says.

Overleaf: Paintings take up an entire wall of an upstairs sitting room and remind Llewellyn of a similar arrangement in his grandmother's sitting room. Rita Thrasher, a self-taught artist from Alabama, painted all the interior room views from photographs; the balloon drawing is by Chris Raschka, and Nina Browne Cassavant painted one of the pastels. A Staffordshire bowl contains eggs Llewellyn and Swenson picked up on their travels, and the miniature ivory and whalebone pieces are from Alaska and Egypt. Llewellyn has owned the reproduction Mottahedeh pitcher since he was a child.

84

At the far end of the living room a pair of ceiling-height, ornately carved Indian teak screens establish a sense of spatial procession. Because of the room's lofty scale, conventionally sized furniture would have felt adrift and diminished, so Mallea and Maloney's choice to make fewer, larger gestures lends a gallerylike air. A Genesee Beer highway billboard from the 1960s—a gift from a house guest—is casually tacked onto the wall opposite the fireplace above an orderly row of Harry Bertoia welded wire chairs and adjacent to Rita Dee's driftwood equine sculpture.

HERMES MALLEA &
CAREY MALONEY

We're the "Buy It Now, Edit It Later" Types

In general, when collectors expand their knowledge and expertise their taste refines exponentially, but not so Carey Maloney. In his case, greater knowledge led to a wider appreciation and a broader appetite, or as he puts it, "the more you know, the more you like, and the more you're itching to buy. Well at least that's how it is with me!" His husband, architect Hermes Mallea, agrees, which is why the immense, 5,500-square-foot basement in their Hudson Valley weekend house resembles a well-ordered prop house. As well as furniture and objects, its thirty-five-year-old accumulation of clippings and auction catalogues provides well-ordered research for the books they both write. Says Maloney, "I guess you could say we're the 'buy it now, edit it later' types."

Upstairs, all the well-edited, spacious rooms contain a random but discriminating inventory that jumps from cartography to Keith Haring to klismos chairs. "Our taste is literally all over the map," says Maloney, who referenced virtually everything he and Mallea own in a book entitled *Stuff*, an interactive series of tutorials on everything from Adivasi terra-cotta to miniature furniture to Chinese scholar's rocks to Ziegler carpets.

Built in the mid-1960s, their ranch house is camouflaged behind green cedar siding, ivy creepers, and pine trees. "I like the fact that it's not an architectural gem," says Maloney, "because first-time guests don't enter with preconceived notions about what should be inside." The front door opens onto a dark entry where a Corimandel screen fronts a coat closet and a sharp left turn leads past a larger-than-life-sized statue of the Greek god Hermes, who's intently focused on a gymnasium-sized room where eighteen-foot-high ceiling rafters support two swings decorated with scenes from the *Kama Sutra*, and a massive stone fireplace consumes four-foot logs. At one end, beyond French doors, a manicured lawn sweeps down to the banks of the Hudson River as well as to a horizon-rich view of the Catskill Mountains.

In the center of the house, Oceanic, African, and Aboriginal art hang above a high, 18-foot-long bar where a former owner, a reputed mobster who affectionately referred to his house as "the Casino," regularly hosted cocktail parties. "The dichotomy of the house's genteel location adjacent to a fifty-acre Italianate mansion and horse farm and its subversive reputation freed us up to have fun with the interior," says Maloney. "We didn't have to be faithful to a period or think about preservation or restoration. We just dealt with the space as it was, pure and simple."

Facing page: Functioning swings flanking the stone fireplace are guest magnets when "big, rocking parties" are in session. Otherwise they serve as a snooze spot for Frankie, a foundling from Atlanta. A teak bed brought in from Kerala is now a sturdy coffee table and displays a two-foot-tall stuffed penguin that formerly belonged to Andy Warhol. Graham Snow's 1948 paint and glitter panel leans on the fireplace mantel above a nineteenth-century American wooden wheel.

Left: In a hallway leading to the master bedroom, a vivid framed poster of Kar-Mi, a Vaudevillian juggler and gun barrel swallower, is paired with an English Gothic Revival chair.

Overleaf, left: In the vestibule a late-nineteenth-century plaster cast of Hermes stands adjacent to a Doug Hill photograph, a taxidermy crow, a floorboard painted with a bucolic scene, and a jointed wood snake cover a glass table. Right: An early-twentieth-century elephant chair, carved from one piece of hardwood, commands a sitting room surrounded by a Charles Dudoydt sideboard, a seventeenth-century Burmese Buddha head, a 1954 pig painting by Bayard Osborn and an ironic, spirited mix of taxidermy.

Maloney grew up in suburban Texas, where "lots of attention was given over to the pursuit of perfection and a Southern finger-bowl civility reigned," and after a stint in the Estate department at Christie's New York, he and Mallea started their own interior design and architecture firm. Mallea grew up in Miami and paid frequent visits to his great-grandparents' house and his large extended family in Cuba. "It was as exotic and sensual as Miami was design-bereft and barren, and the importance placed upon generational nostalgia was palpable," he recalls. "But I think it's safe to say that neither Carey nor I is interested in looking back for its own sake. A historical reference is only relevant if it enhances the present."

Their professional design work invariably relies on big budgets, but personally they don't equate good with expensive. "For us it's 'how' not 'how much' we spend," says Maloney, remembering the time they picked up a Wiener Werkstatte footed vase for next to nothing that coincidentally turned out to be worth a small fortune. "But then we're bottom feeders in comparison to our clients, who are able to buy from the world's great dealers. We're not precious about the things we own. In fact we actively steer clear of pretention. For example, we have rare Aboriginal artifacts but we display them alongside ten-dollar placemats we picked up in the Brisbane airport. It's about decoration and spirit."

Maloney and Mallea think of themselves as house-proud homesteaders. Their weekends revolve around fun and relaxation but they're also happy to host a party for 5 or 150, especially if it benefits a good philanthropic cause. "At one point, when minimalism was having its heyday, I thought we were very old-fashioned because we're very happy to be surrounded by many things and we love them all," says Maloney. "But I actually think minimalism is about denial. It's about a resistance to making a statement. I guess the statement we're making here is that we don't take ourselves seriously!" With that in mind, the first thing Carey remembers purchasing at a very early age at a Texas prison rodeo was a rubber snake, and he now owns around two hundred. And then there's the first piece of taxidermy he ever bought: a century-old pug dog he named Frisky.

JOHN JAY

Connecting an Oreo to a Boot to a Muscle Car

John Jay doesn't really sleep that much. It's a question of time zones and his unquenchable curiosity for the latest and the next. "There's always so much to look at," he says. "I feel as if it's my job to be inspired so that I can be the best I can be." As a partner in Weiden + Kennedy, the acclaimed Portland advertising agency, and the creator of its GX division, Jay commutes between satellite offices in London, Shanghai, Tokyo, and Amsterdam, where he monitors, processes, and interprets each city's cultural pulse. He joined the agency more than twenty years ago without any advertising experience. "I didn't speak English as a kid so I learned key phrases by heart. Automobile language and signage were the first things that appealed," he says, "so I guess that was my advertising apprenticeship." As fate would have it, his visually creative storytelling recently placed him a few names away from the legendary George Lois on an industry list of the most influential art directors of the last fifty years.

Jay grew up in Columbus, Ohio, the eldest son of immigrant Chinese parents, and until he was fourteen the back room of a Chinese laundry doubled as the family's home. "When I tell people I grew up around clothes they assume I was the son of a retailer or a fashion designer, but we literally lived in the room where clothing was hung to dry," he says. In the eighth grade, when he needed a smart outfit for his high school prom, he discretely combed through the racks and borrowed a customer's sweater vest for a few hours. Logic told him to carry a postcard his parents received from Paris around in his pocket so the potency of its image could keep his dream of traveling alive.

Jay views his humble beginnings through a positive lens. "Knowing I wasn't a part of the big world out there pushed me to fantasize, so I was wide-eyed and open to any and every impression," he says. "I was an absolute sponge." College in Ohio first exposed him to European design publications and triggered a passion he's managed to maintain, and he's still likely to stay up into the middle of the night leafing through stacks of art, fashion, design, interiors, and music magazines so long as they fall under the lifestyle rubric. "The best layouts and the best interior design share similar attributes—sidebars, negative space, quotes—whether the vehicle is an object or a typeface," he says. "They're tools to make the eye travel and facilitate the brain's absorption."

Facing page: "All my work is about story-telling," says Jay. A wall in the studio intersperses the 1931 pictorial travel diary of four Japanese boys with a handful of Margaret Keane's wide-eyed Chinatown portraits and a set of pagoda-shaped light fixtures.

Left: Jay's blog postings may locate him in a private karaoke speakeasy, in a studio with beat-box musicians, or in an art salon he's hosting somewhere in the world His favorite artwork is equally eclectic and includes a Shepard Fairey print, a found painting, and a photograph Daido Moriyama took of a pair of fishnet covered legs.

A visual communications degree eventually led to Bloomingdale's hiring him as an art director at a time when far-flung locations and unlimited budgets were the norm. During a rapid, total-immersion crash course in international glamour he got to collaborate with the world's top photographers and models. "Because I never pursued a conventional path in any of my chosen careers, my thinking is free of the standard restraints," he says. "I'm an opportunist in the best sense of the word. I make a habit of walking through open doors."

Jay and his wife, Janet, have a house in Portland, a floating home on the Columbia River, a Manhattan loft, and an 1890s renovated barn in Roxbury, Connecticut. Studio J, their shared workspace in the heart of Portland's old Chinatown, is a visual distillation of all their homes for its mix of Asian and American industrial art, quirky cultural icons, found objects, and strong graphic shapes. Jay equates his lifelong mission to cultivate a highly personal taste with the breadth of his aesthetic appreciation. "Whether it's an Oreo, a boot, a vintage motorcycle jacket, a muscle car, I love anything quintessential, anything with soul," he says. "Narrative is important, so the story behind a creative work matters to me."

Jay disdains the group-grope mentality of the Internet, where virtual experience wins out over the real thing. "Travel was and is my best teacher," he says. "And the connection between authenticity and actually 'being there' will never change no matter how technology advances. It's the difference between observing and participating. It's about getting your hands dirty and living it, and on a more cerebral level it's about comprehending how all the stories in the world weave together."

Jay has an intense dislike of airports but loves hotels, particularly the Tokyo Grand Hyatt, where the high emphasis on service pampers guests as soon as they check in. "Portland is my home base but New York City occupies a big part of my emotional life," he says. "But wherever you feel your most creative, wherever your life story pieces together in the smallest details and the largest expressions, is my definition of home."

94

Left: A Japanese medical figure sits against map art by Wei Wei Dong, an artist based in Shanghai and New York.

Below: These painted cardboards are samples of 1930s Kamishibai, or Japanese paper theater, when storytellers enacted and embodied illustrated images. Considered to be the forefather of all manga art, the colorful boards slid into a wooden box with a curtain to form a stagelike contraption.

Facing page: In one of the many work areas of the studio, a mixed family of metal stools and chairs sits around two long tables where metallic globe lanterns supplement daylight from two walls of windows. A Chinese festival head repainted by a Shanghai graffiti crew sits on the bookcase beneath an evocative bird photograph from Bruce Wolf's Death By Cat series.

Overleaf: Despite its overtly industrial vibe Jay's extracurricular creative studio was conceived as a series of dwelling spaces. "That kind of informality enhances conversations and stimulates ideas," says Jay, "and we want to summon all of our creative forces when we feed the beast of originality."

A vibrant carpet Hume found in Morocco anchors the furniture in a small sitting room. A pair of antique Swedish chairs wear fabric by Dedar, as does the George Smith sofa. Large Vincent Buffile platters sit on a contorted coffee table Hume designed with her husband Frans van der Heijden, whom she describes as a "true renaissance man." The spindly sconces are from Lamp Gras, and the framed artwork leaning on the mantel is the 1962 Chanel couture dress Hume wore to her wedding dinner. "I'm no longer directly connected with fashion," says Hume, whose current wardrobe features Celine, James Perse, Hermès, and Jil Sander, "but I still consider it to be one of the most influential creative arenas."

KATE HUME

Hanging Giant
Crystal Chandeliers
from a Chestnut Tree

Several years ago Kate Hume and her husband, Frans van der Heijden, a Dutch film director and furniture designer, snapped up a seriously dilapidated manor in Cahors, in France's Périgord region, as soon as it came on the market. They'd driven past it dozens of times and tagged it as an ideal vacation home, but due to decades of neglect and spotty renovations its warren of ramshackle rooms was beyond restoration. "It was sorely in need of preservation but it had to be completely reconceived and that's precisely what we found exciting," says Hume, "but everyone else, to a man, thought we were totally mad."

Its now restored stone exterior dates back to the 1700s, and the new white walls and slate floors throughout its interior shell recede to give long-range views of ancient cedars, an orchard, and boxwood allées center stage. Its graphic, contemporary decor is a pithy version of the couple's studio and town house in Amsterdam, both of which are stylistically akin to the well-groomed, art-filled homes Hume designs throughout Russia, America, and Europe. "Old and new is an essential combination in my life and work," she says. "I buy lots of antique furniture but almost always repaint or re-cover it so it feels it's a part of this moment in time."

Full-bodied, peppery wines have a good reputation in this cuisine-rich region, and Hume regularly serves them during the summer months when she entertains outdoors while her husband grills everything from duck to wild mushrooms to bananas. Giant crystal chandeliers become grand wind chimes when she suspends them from the branches of a chestnut tree in a shaded lounge within the formal, parklike grounds.

Hume's parents, who trained as designers and had a very do-it-yourself ethic, might have been prescient when they built their six-year-old future decorator a doll-size replica of their Buckinghamshire house outfitted with replicas of mod furniture. "We didn't have typically English cabbage rose upholstery at home, like a lot of my friends," says Hume. "We had edgier, 1970s stuff."

London was a trend haven during the late 1960s and 1970s, and Hume relished every cult and fad from punk rock to disco, hot pants to maxi dresses. All of it influenced her aesthetic, but none more than Barbara Hulanicki, the creative director of Biba, a Kensington fashion emporium where Twiggy-like customers kitted out in purple lipstick, 1920s cloche hats, bell-sleeved dresses, and lanky platform boots shopped for decadent satin sheets and vases of

Facing page: Hume never cooks but, wine glass in hand, she enjoys observing her husband as he does so. They designed most of the kitchen/dining room furniture, namely a square table, a pair of standing lamps, and an armoire with Hume's sets of *faux bois* that come from Vallauris in southeastern France. "I don't collect vintage things out of nostalgia," she says. "In fact maybe the only time I feel nostalgic is in connection to my kids."

Left: Vallauris ceramics and an artwork after the Expressionist painter Bernard Buffet line the mantel in the small sitting room. Hume defines relaxation as a well-stoked fire and a good book. "Reading is the ultimate antidote to exhaustion for me. Maybe it all started with *Go, Dog. Go!*—in fact, I'm still searching for the tree with the dog party!" she says, laughing. "These days, I like a bit of conspiracy and corruption and I'm a huge fan of Hilary Mantel."

Overleaf: In the main living room the table lamps, console, low chairs, and coffee table are by Heijden Hume. The sofa is George Smith, and the leather double seat is vintage de Sede. The rug is by Golran, the vintage wicker chair came from Holland, and the vintage green painted chair came from Isle-sur-la-Sorgue. The photograph is by the late Dutch photographer Miep Jukkema, who taught Hume new ways of seeing.

ostrich feathers. The store offered up a highly romantic, slightly seditious lifestyle, and Hume and everyone she knew regarded it as a place of pilgrimage.

By the time she came to New York in the early 1980s, she was well versed in the cultural implications of all aspects of design, and Bergdorf Goodman employed her as a trend forecaster. Over the years her appreciation of diverse styles and provenances evolved and deepened to the point where she doesn't favor any one period. "Anything goes," she says, "anything but pastiche, and I sort of run away screaming from anything kitsch, but contradictorily I collect certain ceramics that any sane person might find horrific." From Christophe Côme's Art Deco–inspired molded glass screens to Studio Job's preciously crafted cabinetry, Hume favors the austere as much as the decorative and she layers her interiors accordingly.

By contrast her wardrobe is straightforward and minimal. "My epitome of relaxation is curling up with a good book," she says, "and I look for that level of comfort and informality in my outfits, so it's not just about cut, material, and color, it's whether it allows me to ride my bicycle *and* attend a cocktail party." Hume aims to infuse her interiors with that level of personalization because she's observed how transformative it can be when a home fits its owner like a glove.

Thanks to her clients' healthy budgets, her professional life places her squarely in a world where rare, one-of-a-kind, and bespoke are buzzwords. She's always on the lookout for the unexpected but shies away from anything gimmicky. "Please don't ask me for a life-sized horse with a lampshade on its head or a table lamp that looks like a gun," she says. "My clients are capable of bringing their own sense of humor to a room."

She doesn't see the point of owning anything with a built-in visual obsolescence. "It's why I love color, " she says. "Because it's never passé even though some combinations feel confined to a certain time, which is why I always mix my palettes with modernity in mind. Color is site specific, so the same shade may look glorious in Moscow and fall flat in Paris. Although I take that back—Frans recently bought me a 1986 Mercedes sports car in pistachio and that looks good everywhere."

Facing page: The exposed post-and-beam structure in the attic hallway, where a vintage wardrobe bought in Holland sits next to a prototype bench and stand from Heijden Hume, illustrates the full extent of the detail-oriented, down-to-the-bones renovation. "We did a lot of the invisible stuff like rewiring all the electricity and putting in new plumbing before we could even start with the nice stuff."

Right: In the master bathroom an Albion bathtub and Abyss towels are surrounded by Popham Design's graphically tiled floor. The chairs and jug are vintage finds from Italy. "What enhances my life on a daily basis? Well I would have to say a long soak in a tub," says Hume. "That and sleep, home, my family, and the lovely people I work with. And I mustn't forget my dogs. The late, great Chip and the new princess Liselotte."

Below: Hume lists light, proportion, and flair as the three most important characteristics of a well-designed space, and a guest bathroom on the attic floor—where Kalmar sconces flank a rectangular mirror from Caravane in Paris above a Heijden Hume vanity—fits the bill. "If I were to trace how my interiors style has evolved over the years," she says, "it's becoming less minimal and much more comfortable."

Overleaf: The house has five bedrooms, and in the downstairs master suite the four poster, leaning lamp, desk, and stool are all by Heijden Hume, and the framed drawing is by Richard Nott. As evidenced in the fretwork model of the Eiffel Tower, Hume is attached to Paris. "I also love New York," she says. "After I first saw the movie *Saturday Night Fever* I knew I would have to go there as soon as possible. So I did, and I stayed for nine years."

108

Minutes away from Sunset Boulevard, a
pair of upright Italian ladder-back chairs
from the 1980s and a fantastical, multi-
limbed table by Pedro Friedeberg greet
guests in the entrance hall of Wearstler's
11,000-square-foot Hollywood mansion.
"I'm crazy about his art and sculpture,"
she says of the Mexico-based surrealist,
"and I reconnected with his work during
a collaboration with the architect Ricardo
Legoretta, who is one of his friends.
Whenever I walk into a room I want there
to be a lot to take in. I like a lot of options
for my eyes and my emotions."

KELLY WEARSTLER

Beautiful Imperfection
and a Dialogue
Between Tensions

"Sometimes I'm a 'maximalist,'" says Kelly Wearstler, "but that doesn't hold true across the
board. I'm also paired down, heavy-handed, and restrained. My style runs the gamut." The
other labels she's gathered over the last decade since she started her interior design firm—
"uber," "mega," and "high-chroma"—come and go, but she's consistently credited with single-
handedly reviving Hollywood Regency and lauded as the "new Dorothy Draper." "All and none
of that fits," says Wearstler. "If anything my aesthetic is more European than American."

Wearstler grew up in Myrtle Beach, where her father was an engineer and her mother dabbled
in antiques. She quickly learned the drill and protocol at auctions and thrift shops and was
indoctrinated into Brimfield, the largest outdoor antiques fair in the U.S., at the age of eleven.
"My mother *loved* Americana, which I didn't 'get' at all," she says. "And she was always redecorat-
ing at home, painting rooms different colors and such, so I guess I didn't fall far from the tree!"

She studied graphic design in Boston but switched to interior design because her stamina
couldn't tolerate days of staring into a computer, but she credits a short apprenticeship at
Milton Glaser's studio for infusing her style with its pronounced viewpoint. She subsequently
moved to L.A. hoping to find film set work, and when that didn't pan out she established her
interiors firm with the fee she earned posing as a Playmate of the Month.

The sprawling Beverly Hills estate she shares with her husband, Brad Korzen, and their
sons, Oliver and Eliot, exudes vintage Hollywood allure. In the 1930s, when *Architectural Digest*
profiled its then-owner, actor William Powell, it referred to its movie theater, swimming pool,
manicured gardens, twin tennis courts, and chauffeur's quarters. Wearstler wasn't intimidated
by its glamorous pedigree or its grand scale and never even considered decorating it in period.
"That would have been deadly," she says. "I never overthink things and I never play it safe. If
you don't take risks you don't have a voice. I walked in and my first question was, 'What can
I do to bring this place alive?' I always want to conjure up an emotion. That's how I tap into a
room's essence." Something about this house broke her habit of moving every two years, but
nevertheless she finds herself eagerly anticipating what the next real estate venture will bring.
She predicts something "very, very, very modern," however she chooses to define the term.

Wearstler uses color prolifically, and her palette dances, as one collaborator put it,
"on the edge of Neapolitan abandon." She once striped an entry hall in six different colors and

Facing page: The floor-to-ceiling artwork on the staircase leading down to the media room represents a years-long collection that spans the 1930s to the 1990s. "I'm never drawn to a piece because it's attached to a name. It has to move me first," says Wearstler. "I fall in love with something and then ask about its story."

Left: A Louis Seize railing encircles a vintage chandelier and leads to the master bedroom, while a splayed geometrical pattern on the stair runner echoes the curvature. "I treated the whole space as if you were walking into a painting," she says. "To me the play of opposing forms is intense, contradictory, and harmonious." Guests sometimes assume that Wearstler's two boys graffitied the walls but they actually feature a custom paper.

Overleaf: Wearstler's family often has movie nights and she favors vintage James Bond movies for their sets. A pair of terraced leather sofas Ubald Klug designed for de Sede centrally hold court in the symmetrically appointed media room, where pairs of vintage chairs, domed lamps, torchieres, and demilune tables echo and mirror one another against a backdrop of the casement-windowed room.

immediately realized it was over the top, but apart from that one glitch she's had success by throwing out all the rules, often doing the opposite of popular wisdom. So while a black ceiling is generally thought of as a room's constrictive, dark lid, she perceives it to be a heightening device that makes the ceiling disappear into a void. "Living without color is like living without love," she says. "It's seriously that important. In fact in some rooms it's everything whether it's subtle—one color in different shades or finishes—or all-enveloping."

Art is another transformative feature in her decors. "It's the voice and soul of a room," she says. And while her own collection is peppered with important pieces from recognized artists, she never singles them out or places them prominently, and she never buys according to name. "If I love something it can be a portrait, an abstract, or a photograph," she says. "I'm open to everything. Art helps me to pursue a dialogue between tensions in my work. The last thing I'm striving for is perfection."

She has a wide appreciation for style, so her list of inspirations is long but it focuses on multitalented free spirits from Gio Ponti, Sonia Rykiel, Martin Margiela, and Alexander Wang to Peggy Guggenheim, Doris Duke, Ettore Sottsass, and David Hicks. She currently has lines of clothing, linens, rugs, jewelry, and tableware as well as her own eponymous section in Bergdorf Goodman, where she sells anything that catches her fancy. She doesn't compartmentalize her designs, so a balustrade detail may end up as a bracelet, an element in a painting may evolve into an andiron, a geometric scarf may give birth to a prismatic rug. "It's all of a piece," she says. She inherited Frank, a hundred-year-old family teddy bear, from her grandmother and re-covered him in linen once his fur got loved off. His new, jeweled eyes are buttons from her grandfather's 1930s Navy uniform. "He travels with me, he's my lucky charm. I'm not a fan of flying so if I forget him I think the plane's going down."

Facing page: The Ettore Sottsass totems crown the TV cabinet in the family room, where a rug Wearstler designed anchors a trove of vintage furniture. She holds the flea markets she frequented as a child responsible for her wide-ranging aesthetic and her visceral decision making when she designs and shops. "It's where I learned to think on my feet," she says, "and to make quick decisions before someone else came and snapped up the thing I was after. It taught me to trust my instincts and act decisively."

Below: In Wearstler's library a vintage peacock chair and an Argentinean chandelier rule over an orderly chaos of art, decor, architecture, and fashion books and magazines. "My design process begins with photography, and I take zillions of pictures a week—of anything that inspires me. Life's mix excites me," she says. "Each day my meetings switch from interiors to jewelry, from a hotel to a beach house to my line of housewares or travel accessories."

Above: Original Georgian millwork envelops the master bedroom. Victor Vasarely art hangs above the fireplace, and a 1970s Italian chandelier resembles a curly barrister's wig. The room is equipped with a copper-lined bar, and doors lead to separate his and her dressing rooms. Wearstler's is more than ample and reflects the fact that she's had her eye trained on vintage jewelry, purses, and gloves since she was a teenager. When clients can't decide on the colors they'd like to live with, she often escorts them into their closets to let their clothes speak.

Overleaf: In the dining room a set of ceiling-high French doors spills onto an interior courtyard lined with rows of manicured boxwood topiaries. A giant Sputnik chandelier constructed from an explosion of Lucite rods crowns an assortment of busts, vases, and figurines that landscape a Wearstler-designed cracked glass table, surrounded by curved brass chairs. She never designs grand entrances. "It may not be evident from my work," she says, "but in reality, I'm actually a very shy person."

KENNETH COBONPUE

The Airiness Mimics Sunlight Fracturing Through Trees

When Kenneth Cobonpue's enterprising mother couldn't find appropriate furniture for the houses she designed, she set up a workshop in the backyard of her family home in Cebu, an island in the central Philippines. "I learned how to draw and build from all these incredibly talented craftspeople," he says. "From the earliest age I made operational toy cars, bridges, and nameless machines I'd drop from our balcony to see if they could fly."

After studying in Cebu and Manilla, Cobonpue completed a two-year industrial design course at the Pratt Institute, in Brooklyn. Then in Italy he immersed himself in local artisanal wood and leather crafts and during a stay in Germany he gained firsthand knowledge of business methodology. When he came back to Cebu in 1996, his cross-cultural approach streamlined the family business. "My studies gave me a reverence for the tradition of European artisanship," he says, "but I also have an affinity for Japanese precision and simplicity and I have an affection for New York's edge." Issey Miyake's pleated clothing is also an influence, as is Santiago Calatrava's aerodynamic architecture and Ingo Maurer's poetic, technically innovative lighting.

Cobonpue's Yin & Yang chair—still in production since it brought him international recognition fifteen years ago—has a silhouette that puts to rest the misconception that rattan furniture is a relic of the 1950s. Its simple construction of split rattan wrapped around a gridded steel scaffold and its self-supporting open basket weave are engineered to appear weightless and rock solid at one and the same time. "The airiness in everything I make mimics sunlight fracturing when it hits a grove of trees," he says. "Nature is the ultimate teacher. It's my mentor and adviser." He builds from the ground up and never on a computer because whether a chair sits well is a human subjective not a technical resolution, and if his seating doesn't hug the body it's failing. Working on a computer would also keep him out of contact with the natural materials he uses, including buri and kawayan, both of which have their own particular smell, sound, color, texture, and pliability. "My goal is to tap into the individual character and personality of each fiber and bring out its intrinsic beauty."

Local architects Budji Layug and Royal Pineda built the house where Cobonpue lives with his wife and two children around an existing mahogany and two fifty-foot-high molave trees. They downplayed the site's sloped terrain with terraced landscaping, and exaggerated

Left: The uniformity in furniture and art extends into one of the children's bedrooms, where a Tilt armchair is paired with a framed Alfredo Aquilizan painting. Music is a Filipino family tradition and Cobonpue often sings with his two boys. "I used to listen to jazz and blues all the time when I was driving in the car," he says, "but now, I regret to say, I need that time to make phone calls."

Facing page: In the living room Christy Manguerra's oversize lamp, an assemblage of meticulously folded handmade paper, hovers above deliberately low-slung furniture. French doors lead to a balcony and a view of Cebu, the oldest city in the Philippines. "I love my life here and can never imagine actually leaving it, but if I'm honest I also harbor fantasies about going back to live in the midst of a large city," says Cobonpue, recalling how one of his chair designs was inspired by a dented can of Coke. "I'm not a beach or a moun-tain person but I could see myself retiring to Munich."

it with a splay of cantilevered roofs. In the garden twelve sorts of ferns mingle with tobacco plants, mandevillas, staghorns, Madagascar palms, and agave, and native birds, some endan-gered, live in the canopy. "In nature nothing's superfluous, everything has its purpose," he says, "and that's not a bad mantra!"

Initially all the interior walls were pure white, but their luminescence dramatically intensified the glaring tropical sun. "My wife and I went on a quest to find colors that flat-tered the foliage and neutralized the daylight and found a happy balance in muted browns and vibrant purples," he says. He may have grown up around mid-twentieth-century chairs like Arne Jacobsen's Butterfly and Gio Ponti's Superleggera, but his own home is full of his own designs, and he takes advantage of the resident testers, namely his two teenage sons and a scrappy pair of miniature schnauzers. "The dogs are the ventilation experts. They curl up in anything open weave that lets cool breezes through."

The house's bathrooms incorporate rainwater showers, and an infinity pool cascades down into a lower pool, so guests often liken it to a spa. "I used to be dazzled by ritzy hotels but that's no longer the case since I've lived here. I feel very fortunate," he says. "We're definitely in a sort of oasis here and sometimes it's as if time has stopped. Maybe that's why, these days, I'm drawn to exotic places like Nepal, Burma, Peru, Turkey, and Egypt, where people still wear traditional garb and they're not glued to cell phones."

There are more than 7,000 islands in the Philippine archipelago, and Cobonpue likes to explore them on weekends in one of several of his classic sports cars. He has two 1956 Jaguar XK140s, a 1961 Jaguar E-Type, a 1959 Porsche 356, and his favorite, a 1974 Ferrari Dino. "They all have a no-frills construction. No electronic gadgetry. No sign of plastic in the interi-ors," he says. "They're all leather, wood, and steel." His childhood preoccupation for building vehicles has endured although the contraptions have evolved into sleek concept electric cars, one of which is a cross between a hybrid skateboard and a recumbent bicycle. Needless to say, he no longer drops anything off the balcony to test whether it's capable of flying.

Above: The house is comprised of several pavilions whose sloping roofs resemble the architectural massing of a traditional Asian temple where concrete steps ascend and hover above a reflecting pool in front of the entrance. "Birds seem to love the garden as much as we do, and I guess the positioning of all the water elements constitutes good feng shui, but we didn't incorporate any of those principles when we built the house," says Cobonpue. "We just followed our instincts about serenity and beauty."

Facing page: A covered patio by the swimming pool affords cool breezes, and a sculptural spiral staircase winds up to the master bedroom.

Overleaf: The dining room windows look onto the city as well as a mature bamboo grove, and the cross ventilation provides a tree-house feel. The six hanging pendants are from Danny Fang's Checkmate series, the artwork is by Charlie Cho, and the table is constructed from solid French walnut. Aluminum threaded curtains help temper streams of morning sunlight.

"I'm more fluent with photography than I am with painting," says Ledbetter, "and in recent years I've become more interested in specific photographers. I keep up with their portfolios, and even though I may not have met them there's a personal-relationship aspect to my collection. I'm not motivated by investment—it's all about admiration for the work." Artists on the salon wall include Aaron Siskind, Margaret Sartor, John Patrick Salisbury, Robert Motherwell, Horace Bristol, Jacqueline Humphries, Robert Gordy, Michael Kenna, William Gedney, and John Dugdale. "I mean, the quality of light in some of Dugdale's work, or Nan Goldin's for that matter, is like Vermeer!"

LEE LEDBETTER

Perfect, Skillfully Executed Interiors Leave Me Cold

Lee Ledbetter was born in Monroe, a pretty Louisiana city where low-slung ranches wear Palladian drag and perfectly proportioned Georgian houses claim the land between rivers and bayous. In the midst of such scenic beauty his yearning for a tropical climate prompted him to memorize the entire Hawaiian alphabet and cultivate varieties of banana and papaya plants in a makeshift backyard greenhouse. "It was tough growing up gay in a football town," he says, "so I identified with exotic vegetation, which I guess is more than slightly Freudian!"

When he wasn't outside in nature shimmying up trees, scavenging birds' nests, or digging for arrowheads, he collected city maps. "I drew ridiculously large house plans," he remembers. "Not elevations but plans where each room looked onto a courtyard, a stretch of water, or a beach lined with billowing palms." Once he hit eighth grade he sat in on some of the consultation meetings his mother had with her interior designer and remembers showing up to one of them with a page torn out of *Architectural Digest*. "Boy, was I precocious. I was rearranging my room every six months at that point and I'd found a geometric carpet—it may have been in a story about Gloria Vanderbilt—that matched a black-and-white optical theme I'd devised to show off my Age of Aquarius black light posters."

In his teens he took tons of art classes, and when he realized he lacked the courage to pursue a living as a painter he shifted his interests to architecture. After he earned a master's degree at Princeton he built up a stellar résumé with Robert A. M. Stern and Gwathmey Siegel in New York, Michael Graves in Princeton, and Skidmore Owings and Merrill in Chicago before going off on his own. "If I were more business savvy I would have opened an office in Atlanta," he says, "but I really feel at home in New Orleans. I get so much pleasure from its history and its gritty texture. If ever I need to cure a bad mood I just go for a stroll." The city's Caribbean climate and lush vegetation is also a major plus. "We're so in touch with nature here. I mean ferns grow out of cracked mortar, and cat's claw ivy vines devour entire blocks. The canopy of live oaks keeps the sky off limits and I love that. It's like living in a womb."

The 1955 house Ledbetter shares with Douglas Meffert, an environmentalist who heads the Louisiana Audubon Society, is near the river on an elevated plot. Occupying 2,200 square feet, it's clad in vertical redwood siding and contains a tailored assortment of mid-twentieth-century furniture, contemporary photography, abstract art, muscular ceramics, and muted,

Facing page: "Color needs a lot of visual space, and I'm happier living within a limited palette. I once had a client who asked for rooster colors, and that was pretty excruciating for me because what's tried and true in one place falls apart in another," says Ledbetter. In his dining room a Saarinen table sits on a 1920s Oushak carpet surrounded by nineteenth-century French Napoleon III chairs. The ceramic centerpiece is by Peter Lane, the glass chandelier is 1950s Murano, and the painting, entitled *Day And Night; Day And Night*, is by Emily Sartor.

Right: On a Karl Springer étagère from the 1980s, Russel Wright ceramics for Bauer share space with a Reed & Barton "Diamond" silver coffee/tea set and a porcelain skull by Nymphenburg.

nineteenth-century Oushak carpets similar to the kind Ledbetter grew up with. "I go for all periods of antiques, ancient and modern, providing there are great lines and elongated legs," he says. "I have zero interest in furniture that's currently made. It has no proven track record."

His preferred color palette is "very Halston—black, white, brown, beige, and gray," he says. "I shy away from anything stronger because I know I can't tolerate it for very long, and believe me I've tried." When he first moved into the French Quarter he went completely wild and paired a bright yellow Adam Fuss photograph with a saffron V'Soske rug and a blue vinyl sofa. But after a while it felt as if it were fighting for his attention. His favorite architecture is stripped-down classicism or spare Renaissance, and whenever he visits Les Invalides in Paris he feels as if he's walking through a massing model because its planes and volumes turn space into a tactile object. He has the same visceral connection to the Santa Maria della Consolazione pilgrimage church in Todi.

"Maybe it's a prerequisite for living in New Orleans but I'm attracted to imperfection. I have little time for cool minimalism," he says. "A skillfully executed interior leaves me cold. I can forget it in a minute." Applying that sensibility to art, he is drawn to work where there is some element left unresolved. "Maybe it's a hair of a degree away from being ugly so it feels almost organic and sublime like nature. To me there's calm beneath the surface of that kind of tension."

Ledbetter just purchased his embodiment of perfection in the form of a two-door 1970 Mercedes-Benz 280 SL with a concave hardtop, popularly called a Pagoda. "Every car from that period is a rough bucket," he says, "so it's not about comfort. It's about experiencing what it feels like to be inside an intricate mechanism, like a vintage watch. It's about sitting inside a time capsule with a leather interior."

Right: In a hallway that backs onto the dining room, an untitled photograph by Todd Hido is given pride of place. "I love crusty pieces, which is why I love old rugs," he says. "I would much rather have a carpet that's been handmade by a tribe and used for a hundred years than something new, but maybe it's because I grew up with them."

Below: Imaginary buildings that Ledbetter designed as a child had futuristic, needle-shaped towers and rotating restaurants, but he grew up to be a preservationist. In the living room a Pamela Sunday ceramic sculpture sits on a table Ledbetter designed. The side table is Paul McCobb, the chairs are T. H. Robsjohn-Gibbings, the lamp is by James Mont, the photograph of a palm tree is by Jack Pierson, and the photograph beneath the skylight is by David Hilliard. The rug is nineteenth-century Oushak.

Facing page: "I'm as at ease with interior design as I am with architecture, and as far as I'm concerned they're two sides of the same professional coin," he says. "You can't isolate one process from the other when you design a room." A view toward the living room fireplace shows the surround flanked by a pair of Peter Lane's ceramic sculptures as well as an Edward Wormley sofa, a large painting by George Dunbar, and a smaller painting by the California painter John Sonsini.

Overleaf, left: A Hiroshi Sugimoto photograph hangs adjacent to the living room's grand piano and a ceramic sculpture by Eva Hild. "I fell in love with Hild's work as soon as I discovered it," he says. "In fact, I don't know how you couldn't love it." Right: In the master bedroom an Edward Wormley headboard is paired with Paul McCobb side tables and a 1950s Baker chair. The photograph over the bed, *Iceberg #30, Disko Bay, Greenland, 2000,* is by Lynn Davis; Tom Baril's *Dahlia* leans against the wall beneath Bill Jacobson's *Song of Sentient Beings #1633.*

In Skouras's living room a chandelier she designed presides over a menagerie of furniture and accessories, including a bespoke chaise by Alannah Currie that incorporates a mute swan with a World War I army tent; a Victorian taxidermy ibis circa 1865; a pair of Rougier cockatiel lamps; a Buccellati wine cooler used as a planter; and an obscured 1927 oil painting by Guy Bardone. "When I create rooms for clients I'm more restrained," she says. "Slightly more restrained."

MARJORIE SKOURAS

Dressing Dinner Tables from Target and Tiffany's

"I come from a long line of bawdy women, and the current batch all seem to be interior designers," says Marjorie Skouras, referring to herself, her mother, and two sisters. All four use color focally and at times judiciously, but Skouras has the capacity to go truly wild. "I've always thought more is best. In fact, if I had my way, everyone would have at least one red room." As a testament to this outlook, in one of her more highly published projects she painted the sixteen-foot-high living room walls of a 1920s Mediterranean-style villa an outrageous scarlet pink. And because restraint is not one of her traits, she then rattled the monotone of its formal garden with a lineup of purple ruffled umbrellas and paid tribute to *Edward Scissorhands* in the master suite with a four-poster bed she concocted out of giant fake boxwood topiaries. "I'm comfortable working in all periods and styles but not in a straightlaced way. I need to apply my own, shall we say, twist."

As Skouras recalls, her mother's decorating career began as a means to pay for her eleven-year-old daughter's horse tack, but prior to that the family kept in-house decorators from Gumps department store on retainer. "A mysterious crew of people regularly swooped in and redid our house from soup to nuts," she says. "I'd come back from school and everything would be completely transformed. It was dramatic and exciting."

A fourth-generation San Franciscan, Skouras spent close to two decades on the production side of the movie industry after she earned an art history degree at UCLA. In addition to interior design she also has a studio line of chandeliers and tables she encrusts with blizzards of jade, lapis lazuli, agate beads, amethyst nuggets, fossilized black coral, or abalone shells.

Built in 1925, her current house in Los Angeles's Beachwood Canyon sits in a "staunchly Bohemian enclave" of actors and costume designers, none of whom were particularly fazed by recent reports of a seven-foot-long adult Puma loose in the hills between their street and the legendary Hollywood sign. Apart from keeping her two miniature Dachshunds, Georges Pompidou and Sultana, under surveillance, Skouras also took it in stride. "Maybe," she says, "we've all seen *Bringing Up Baby* too many times?"

The house is composed of style-driven vignettes, none more interactive than the dining room, where the walls are covered with blackboard paint. "Everyone who enters is invited to contribute some graffiti with the caveat not to disturb what already exists," she says, "and

Left: A not particularly formal table setting centers around a solid silver sculpture by Eric Goulder, an engagement present from her husband. "He's divine," she says of them both. Bennington Potters side plates form a family with Williams-Sonoma fish bowls, D.L. & Co. malachite plates, Buccellati flatware, and vintage abalone salt cellars on fabric from Tony Duquette's silk collection for Jim Thompson.

Facing page: In a sitting room off the kitchen, one of Skouras's honeycomb lanterns hangs over her Moorish-inspired table and an L-shaped banquette that's multilayered with custom pillows. Most of the artwork is also Skouras's, including a central portrait of her beloved dog Georges Pompidou.

there's absolutely no editing on our part." Alongside a chalky portrait of her daughter, India, and quotes by everyone from Einstein to Rita Hayworth, a perennial favorite is, "No more taupe," as well as the motto *du jour*: "Be the kind of woman who, when your feet hit the floor in the morning, the Devil says, 'Oh crap, she's up!'"

Since the early 1980s, when she first fell in love with Halcyon boxes, Skouras has consistently collected a broad range of things from taxidermy to anything malachite, but in the last couple of years her acquisitive days have begun drawing to a close. "I don't actively need anything," she says, "unless it's unusual or unless I feel compelled to create it myself."

She looks to nature and travel whenever she's lacking creative juice and admires the French decorator Madeleine Castaing, who walks the shaky stylistic line between kitsch and chic. The extraordinary tastemaker Tony Duquette was one of her idols—she beams when she recalls meeting him when she was ten—for the way he created opulence out of found objects. Skouras is likewise a fierce believer in unpredictable and uninhibited stylistic marriages. "If it works I'll put a museum relic next to something from IKEA. I see no correlation between elegance and price. It's all a point of view, a state of mind," she says. "Whenever I can I opt for the highest quality, but I'm prone to dress tables with everything from Target to Tiffany's."

Skouras and her financier husband, Bruno Bardavid, prepare all the family meals together and finger food for fifty might include foie gras directly off the plane from Paris, a tarot card reader, and a jazz piano and guitar ensemble made up of close friends. Above all else Skouras wants guests to feel relaxed when they enter her home. "I think there's a conveyed sense of fun and a sense of 'wow' here," she says. "It's clearly not everyone's cup of tea, but hopefully the delight and joy we derive from living with equal amounts of drama and glamour comes across. Most people we know share our belief that life isn't a dress rehearsal." Or to put it in the words of Mame Dennis, her favorite movie character, life is a banquet.

Facing page: Doors lead to a sunlit courtyard off the living room, where a 1930s Savonarola chair by Addison Mizner accompanies Skouras's three-sided malachite table and a three-arm standing Spanish Revival lamp beneath a wall of artworks by Ellsworth Kelly, Claes Oldenburg, and Imogen Cunningham.

Below: Artist Alison Sprague painted the house's entry door and Skouras topped it off with a vintage French door knocker. The chandelier is by Philippe Starck. Skouras customized the umbrella stand and festooned the closet doors with moss and gemstone beetle hardware.

Right: In the master bedroom a 1950s Suzani tapestry backs the Skouras-designed headboard and bed linens. During the daily housekeeping the sheets and pillowcases are sprayed with clementine or rosemary oil. "I was sixteen when I decorated my own bedroom," she remembers. "I covered one side of a bamboo screen in Fortuny fabric, and I still have it."

Overleaf, left: A dining room vignette formed around Skouras's malachite mirror, cast coral candlesticks, and an eighteenth-century console includes Cecil, a taxidermy Red McCaw, and a Victorian dome of taxidermy birds. She attributes one of her favorite aphorisms, "Logic will get you from A to B. Imagination will take you everywhere," to Albert Einstein. Right: Persephone, a taxidermy peacock, perches on Skouras's Oyster bar surrounded by Mathieu Lustrerie crystal beetle wall lights, Philippe Starck Kong chairs, Eric Goulder's vellum artist proofs, and a giant clamshell filled to the brim with rough-cut rock crystals. "When I work for myself I have creative carte blanche and recently that fact has put a damper on me designing interiors. I don't miss being responsible for other people's money."

142

"When I first arrive," says Mathieu, "I take a deep breath and inhale all the clarity of the space—it opens my mind. Then I go upstairs to the roof and take the pulse of the city." Music by Bach, Glenn Gould, Arvo Pärt, and Léo Ferré keeps him grounded, and whenever he needs a jolt of color he takes a glimpse at his current favorite film, Jean-Luc Godard's *Le Mépris*, which is permanently installed on his iPhone.

PAUL MATHIEU

Happiness Is a
4B Pencil and a Blank
Piece of Paper

Paul Mathieu may have a trace of Bedouin, nomad, or gypsy blood for the way he matter-of-factly owns homes that are oceans apart in France, America, and India. At a time when long security lines and epic delays deter the most seasoned of travelers, Mathieu still gets excited before each trip. "As soon as I take my seat on a plane I'm relaxed and in my element," he says. "There's something appealing about forward motion. It leads to new ideas and new perspectives."

As a child growing up in a small village outside of Lyons, grand-scale journeys weren't part of the picture, but his mother regularly took side trips to neighboring villages. "When she went to her cheese or poultry suppliers she often came back with furniture," he recalls. "She discovered things—in the back of a barn or in a shed—that other people didn't value or had forgotten about and she restored them and gave them new life."

Mathieu attended the Ecole des Beaux Arts in Lyons and subsequently studied in England before he took off to L.A. with visions of David Hockney swimming pools and lawn sprinklers in his head. There he met designer Michael Ray, who became his life and work partner for fourteen years. In the 1980s, after style doyenne Andrée Putman commissioned a Mathieu and Ray furniture collection, the duo commuted between Aix en Provence and Paris as press-anointed charter members of the "nouveau baroque" movement. "I'm attached to New York," says Mathieu, who moved to Harlem in 2000. "It's the most spontaneous city I know, a veritable creative incubator." It's also where he maintains his largest body of work—furniture collections for industry titans Stephanie Odegard, Ralph Pucci, and Holly Hunt.

In sharp contrast to his sparsely furnished uptown apartment, his atelier in Aix is layered with twenty years' worth of prototypes and sketches. In an even sharper contrast the Udaipur *haveli* he acquired a handful of years ago, while spending stretches of time in Rajasthan designing Jali-work furnishings with local craftsmen, is almost monklike. The alchemy of Jali, where chunks of solid marble are transformed into paper thin, lacy structures, strikes Mathieu as poetical. "This idea of chipping away at any material until you discover its essence or inner life is a wonderful metaphor," he says. "It's what I already do with wood and bronze." Over the course of the three-year renovation, with a bevy of artisans permanently on hand, Mathieu could easily have sprinkled in a few showy architectural statements and altered the simple complexion of

Facing page, above: The entry to the house is at street level and a no-shoes policy allows guests to appreciate the constantly cool floors. Mathieu restored the hand-carved teak doors on every floor and large, potted plants are rotated inside and out depending on the weather. Below: In the second-floor living room the floors and walls are all finished with coats of coconut oil and a final layer of agate stone that hardens over time. Mathieu designed the chairs and Jali table, and the textile is a part of his collection of embroideries and vintage saris. The amber-colored Murano glass in the array of windows casts a golden light that's often burningly intense.

Left: During the renovation, while he contemplated how he could open up the house's warren of rooms, Mathieu discovered beautifully carved stone pieces that are at least two hundred years old. They inspired Mathieu to experiment with traditional floral imagery.

the thirty-year-long abandoned building but instead he downplayed the use of ornamentation and settled for a series of unassuming spaces. Each one relates or directly connects to a central inner courtyard where terraced pots of night-blooming jasmine thrive throughout monsoon season and give off their sensual fragrance when darkness falls. Hand-chiseled stone covers all the floors, and light bounces and reflects off the ivory-colored walls.

The house has no formal dining room and relatively few chairs, so when he's in residence he may serve up a coq au vin and scotch or a vegan onion tart to guests seated on a khadi rug. Apart from the kitchen and bathroom, none of the spaces have any assigned purpose, so there are no predictable furniture configurations and Mathieu stores away nonessentials in trunks in the cellar. "I've gotten into a habit of giving away any clothes I haven't worn in over six months because I don't want my life complicated, and here I feel placated when surfaces are clear and uncluttered. I like to be flexible and adapt to any situation so owning indispensible things doesn't really make much sense," he says. "I've trained myself to focus on whatever's directly in front of me even when I'm in the midst of total chaos, so just give me a 4B pencil and a blank piece of paper and I'm happy."

Apart from a few ancient carved stones uncovered during the renovation, Mathieu designed everything in the house. On his spare desk are sketches of vitrines and elevations of an opulent private museum in Jaipur, a future home for a client's lifelong collection of textiles, rare enameled boxes, and Mughal jewelry. A few times a week Mathieu rides his Honda 250 motorcycle past an exotic lake hotel and continues outside the city to the hillside Ubeshwar Ji Mahadev Temple, dedicated to the Hindu god Shiva. "I don't associate extravagance with lavishness and tons of money. I associate it with light, visual space, and time to think. Being able to look and think without the bombardment of noise is luxurious," he says. "I haven't found my true home yet. Maybe I'm still looking. Or maybe my home is with me wherever I am."

Left: In the bathroom an ebonized table Mathieu designed for Odegard holds a stack of cotton towels. The bath utilizes solid stone slabs, and an intricately carved block of stone functions as a step. "There are three water spouts rather than one, so it feels like a fountain more than a traditional tub," he says. Filled to the brim with cold water, during the too-hot weather months it's an ideal place to cool off.

Facing page: Mathieu was an acquisitive teenager. He frequented auctions and mainly bought furniture with his pocket money, including a Louis XVI chair his sister still owns. The *haveli*'s ground floor sitting room is softly furnished and prompts instant relaxation and lounging. The sills of its wall nooks are kept clear so their variously deep recesses can act as light repositories.

Overleaf: Mathieu created a wide skylight on one side of the living room where prototype chairs and a pair of bronze dogs are the minimal accompaniments to one of his ebonized tables. Perceptibly, the room comes across as a symmetrical composition of niches, but only one of them is permanently occupied with a photograph of a bucolic landscape.

The interior volume of the house is 2,300 square feet, and Siskin relished the idea of having more windows than wall space because he owns relatively little art. He amassed a candlestick collection over a number of years; the designer of the 1960s steel and mahogany dining table is unknown, the chairs are 1950s French, and the chandelier is bronze and was manufactured in India.

PAUL SISKIN

One Aspic Away from Throwing a Big Dinner Party

As a teenager growing up in Beverly Hills, Paul Siskin routinely snuck onto movie lots. "The facade aspect of the sets totally fascinated me," he says. His family manufactured mass-market furniture, so the decor in his home was cozy, "very Ozzie & Harriet with acorn finials everywhere, and somewhere between the fantasy of Hollywood and the stark reality of my parents' business I decided to become a decorator." When he delivered the news, an uncle's reaction was flat. "Your father would roll over in his grave," he said. "We hire decorators. We don't become one of them!"

Siskin eventually moved to New York, studied at Parsons, and found employment with John Saladino, who was then at the height of his career. "I loved every minute of it," says Siskin. "I would have done it for free. His classicism, historical references, sense of color, and phenomenal editing is still with me, but our attitudes are very different. John is an artist painting a canvas; I'm a tool in the sense that I enable people to paint their own canvas. My favorite homes aren't put together by decorators, they're created by people who have the confidence to run with their own style."

From the earliest age Siskin planned to build his own house. "In my mind," he says, "it always had high ceilings and glass walls and sat on top of a hill overlooking the San Fernando Valley. I ended up building exactly that but on the east coast in the Hudson Valley." Located on four mountainous acres, the 2,300-square-foot house is all stucco and plate glass. It has Palladian proportions, a Mies van der Rohe sensibility, and a laid-back grandeur thanks to Joan Chan, a dear friend, who collaborated on its architecture and interior millwork. "It took forty-five years to plan and five years to build," says Siskin, downplaying the calamitous, glacial pace of the construction process that often made him feel like the protagonist in the movie *Mr. Blandings Builds His Dream House.*

In one stark case of denial he even tried to move in when construction was nowhere near finished. "I was boasting to friends that I was an aspic short of hosting a big dinner party," he says, "because the reality—it was a money pit and it was months away from completion—was just too painful to bear." That's when he christened the house "Brokeback Manor." When he finally got the contractor's permission to clear out gangs of sawhorses and ladders, he brought in a collection of books, furniture, and objects amassed over forty years, and he was "at home"

Facing page: A Le Corbusier chair sits beneath a Lynn Davis photograph, next to a floor lamp Siskin designed and a nineteenth-century English trivet table. "In any place I live I'll never consider it to be 'finished' and that's the apex of luxury for me," he says. "Professionally I'm always up against deadlines. The informal way I live matches my work so I tend to develop close, lifelong friendships with my clients."

Right: Siskin, a voracious reader, likes to work in bed. "Maybe it's because I've lived so long in a small city apartment, but I like talking on the phone when I'm extremely comfortable." In one of the guest bedrooms a tabletop arrangement attests to Siskin's sense of irony. As does his way of referring to the smallest guest room as the "lesser VIP suite."

overnight without any discernible period of adjustment. Sad to say, shortly thereafter Sisken sold the house in order to compensate for the inflated budget, but he's thrilled that he executed the house of his dreams.

Despite his fully equipped, professional-looking kitchen, Siskin never cooks. "I admit it," he says. "I select my dinner guests according to their culinary skills." A pocket door separates the living room from a sitting room where he slept on a daybed. "The chief function of the other furniture in that room, the desk and chairs, is to receive my clothes when I take them off and throw them in their direction." The panoramic view from his bed stretches into the Berkshires and affords frequent sightings of bald eagles, deer, wild turkey, foxes, and bears.

All of Siskin's belongings, including those in his Manhattan apartment, show signs of age. "Timelessness is a characteristic of good design," he says. "New, new, new has no soul." In his mind an upholstered chair looks infinitely better when it's cradling a snoozing dog, and he welcomes scratches and wine bottle rings on his dining table. "When an object shows no signs of use it might as well be in storage. Anything you use to feather your nest reciprocates the energy you've invested." When he reupholstered his Corbusier Petit Confort chair after thirty-five years, he chose red suede, a fabric he always warns clients against because it's so impractical, but personally he can indulge because newness is not a quality he's striving for. According to Siskin concrete floors are the most forgiving surfaces, which is why he used them throughout the house to unite all of the rooms. "Although it's not without its shortcomings. The survival rate for dropped cell phones is virtually nil. But, boy, is it worth it."

Facing page: A nineteenth-century desk adjacent to Siskin's bedroom displayed a large collection of laboratory glass. The oversize lamp is 1950s French and the chair is American from the 1960s. "Taste is so subjective," he says. "I have a friend whose decor is tacky and wild and I love it because I love her. I would hate it if we all had a shared aesthetic or if we all succumbed to only buying fashionable things, whatever that means."

Right: An 1800s Italian Bergere chair sits next to a sculptural tub in the master bathroom. "There's a big difference between fantasy and fact when you create an interior. In theory it would be fun to design a movie set, but it goes against my instincts because I'm trained to build places people actually inhabit."

Below: An 1800s English wall clock hangs above a 1920s painted pine bench. Siskind mounted an industrial 1950s mirror above a marble sink designed by Joan Chen. "The longer I live, the more I want to pare down," he says. "One of the good things about aging is not having anything to prove."

Overleaf: In the living room, Joan Chen designed the steel fireplace, and the buttery yellow leather chairs are from B&B Italia. The rug is by Patterson, Flynn & Martin; a machine mold leans on the mantel alongside Elsa Peretti candlesticks; and a French 1950s leather settee sits perpendicular to a long linen sofa from Restoration Hardware. "Relaxation and comfort are prime words for me."

Wolfson picked up a set of eight T-chairs designed in the 1950s by Katavolos, Kelly & Littell, and one of them sits in his studio on a 1960s Danish carpet beneath a photograph by Iran Issa Khan. Various study models and framed working drawings demonstrate how his furniture is not preoccupied with function. "I'm not sure why a creative person would want to rehash something that already exists," he says. "Everything I make has its own narrative. They're characters in their own right."

PHILIP MICHAEL WOLFSON

I'm a Minimalist at Heart but I Need to Touch Everything

Most of the sculptural objects Philip Michael Wolfson designs appear to capture or suspend motion. A desk mimics a kind of twisted trajectory; a chair jostles with itself; a white table base conjures up a stream of heavy cream. Wolfson's father was a space scientist, which may or may not account for his son's attraction to the hovering and airborne, but Wolfson sees the shapes he designs as the outcome of his efforts to coax out each material's latent characteristic force. Either way, some of his furniture has enormous grace and some of it looks downright aggressive. "I want my objects to be felt rather than easily heard," he says. "That's a paramount concern."

Born in Philadelphia, Wolfson subsequently moved with his family to Washington, D.C., Los Angeles, Miami, and New Orleans. Two anchoring memories from those transient years are his extensive set of Lego and his well-serviced fleet of modern toys cars. During that period of time he also discovered he had a fascination with the way other people lived. "I developed a habit of running through any homes we visited so I could memorize the layout before we left," he says, "and I set off many alarms in the process and caused my mother great embarrassment." He began collecting at the age of twelve when he successfully bid on a set of Art Deco silverware, a garbage pail, and a bed frame in an auction commemorating the decommission of the *Queen Mary*. Later he amassed piles of vintage publications from the 1900s through the 1930s and recalls dog-earing the pages of the real estate sections of *Town & Country* magazine, where they published apartment floor plans.

After studying architecture at Cornell, he transferred to the Architectural Association, in London, where a tutor, Zaha Hadid, collared him to head the design department of her then-fledgling architectural practice. The manipulated motion inherent in her horizontal skyscrapers and topographic furniture struck Wolfson as a natural extension of the mid-twentieth-century Russian Constructivism and Italian Futurism he was drawn to, and he stayed with Hadid through the 1980s.

The furniture in his current portfolio relies on a wide range of materials including colored aluminum, carbon fiber, acrylic stone, concrete canvas, cast bronze, and Corian, and his inspiration can be as prosaic as origami or the letter Q or as esoteric as the sound waves of

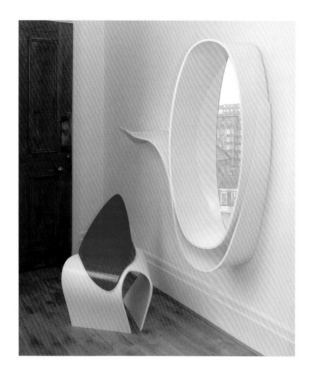

Left: In the entrance to Wolfson's studio and living space two pieces from his Twisted series are constructed from acrylic stone. The shape of his Whynot mirror derives from the letter "Q" as it morphs into a spiral. His strawberries and cream Split chair LOW features a compound twist and an uncharacteristically bold use of color. "Visual movements project certain colors to me," he says. "That's why I was commanded to use red here."

Facing page: In the studio the Arkana table and chairs date back to the 1960s, the carbon fiber centerpiece vase is a recent studio prototype, the seascape video is by Maxim Nilov, the Tsukumogami stool is another studio piece, and the double-stacked aluminum Tonic tables are late 1990s prototypes. "I designed a rather large table for someone several years ago," he says, "and they've taken this thing with them through four different moves, even when they downsized. That's terrifically rewarding for me to know that something I created is that well appreciated."

poured whiskey. "I always come at things from an architectural perspective because I'm fusing art and design into a kind of sculptural exploration," he says. "Function and usability come later, if at all. Comfort's a relative concept."

Wolfson surely shares the family genes of an uncle whose prolific collection of textiles, objects, and ephemera from the first half of the twentieth century now comprises much of the collection of the Wolfsonian, a museum in the heart of South Beach, Miami. "Acquisition is definitely in my blood, however I'm currently not in the market for anything," he says. "I have no more space and no more need!" Although once in a while he finds himself on the lookout for Marcello Fantoni's ceramics from the 1950s, and he recently purchased fifty-three pieces of the *faux bois* pottery produced by Grandjean Jourdan in Vallauris, France. "I don't attach a nostalgia or a longing for the past to any of the vintage things I own, and at this point in my life I'd rather look forward than backward."

He keeps an apartment in Miami, but his home and studio occupy the top floor of a late-nineteenth-century house in a mansion block in Bayswater, within sight of the heart of London's financial district. His designs may rely heavily on negative space but his apartment is chock-full. "At heart I'm a minimalist," he says. "But in reality I need to touch and see everything I own. I derive a great deal of enjoyment from my belongings. For example, I have a Gio Ponti side table that absolutely hits all the right buttons. It embraces shadow and reflection, plays with light, affects the space around it, and it's always a pleasure to be around."

Wolfson prefers rhythmically complex music, from Baroque to Brazilian salsa, but its floridity never seeps into his work. "My sense of color," he says, "has been referred to as 'bland' and 'odd,' so it was reassuring to be asked, as I was recently, to forecast trends for the coming year." His non-use of applied pattern is pretty rigid, although he once relented and inserted a swatch of eighteenth-century Toile de Jouy in a bed headboard in a historically correct project. A current project involves his applying graffiti and written abstractions onto a series of concrete canvas sculptures. "It's my way of referencing the spirit that inhabits inanimate objects."

Above: A variation of a sectional sofa Wolfson used in a series of interior design projects in the 1990s converses with a pair of flamed mahogany Cubist cabinets from the same period. On their shelves and sitting on the Tsukumogami Soul stool are some of Wolfson's Faux Bois Vallauris ceramics from the 1950s, while a 1960s Gambone vase sits on the floor.

Facing page: "Fashion doesn't influence me at all. Not one bit. Oscar Niemeyer is one of my gods and so many other peoples' aesthetics influenced me. There's Zaha [Hadid], of course, all the Futurists, and the Russian contributions to the Constructivist movement," he says. "Then there's Luciano Baldessari and artists like Naum Gabo, Lucio Fontana, and Mathias Goeritz . . . the list goes on." In the dining area more T-chairs sit around an Italian glass table on a Scandinavian carpet from the 1960s. One of Wolfson's Tsukumogami Flowers acts as a centerpiece while its Mushroom and Flower counterpart sits on the floor.

"The way I set out the objects in this place has nothing to do with shock value," says Azoulay. "It's about having a dramatic base whose relaxed intensity allows me to move slowly through the world with great intent, like a coyote." In the apartment's utilitarian stainless steel and teak kitchen, *Protractor Face*, an Irving Penn photograph, supervises a traveling confessional and a wooden farm chair that a previous owner stabilized with twisted wire.

RAY AZOULAY

If Comfort's a Top Priority You're in the Wrong Place

Obsolete, Ray Azoulay's California antique store, is hard to categorize. Located in Venice in a former rosewater distillery, it's a living, breathing example of why online, virtual shopping ranks as a sensory-deprived activity. The cavernous space is filled with centuries- and decades-old generic relics whose rarity, patina, or mere survival elevates them to demented luxury status: articulated mannequins, weathered medicine bags, stuffed foxes, industrial lighting, splattered painter's easels, Mexican *santos*, a convent refectory table, military watches. "If physical comfort's a priority," he says, "you're in the wrong place."

A few blocks away, above a row of cafés whose surfboard vibe strikes Azoulay as "East Village with an ocean," his quirky condominium is a distilled incarnation of the store minus its fragrance, dim lighting, and hypnotic sound system. The 1,800-square-foot space, designed by architect Michael Sant, spreads over two floors in railroad arrangements and is naturally lit by a glass-walled interior courtyard.

Azoulay grew up on Long Island, a sixty-minute drive from Manhattan. "It might as well have been four thousand miles away," he says, "because we saw the city as a dangerous place. We came in once a year to see the Christmas tree in Rockefeller Center and quickly rushed back to safety." His mother was literally a homemaker and thought nothing of jack hammering a wall to expand a room. "I inherited an amazing amount of confidence from her. She taught me to trust my own instincts and to not fear drastic change, and that proves invaluable to me every day in the store. Of course it helps that her renovations always turned out well."

After fourteen years of casting his net wide and far, Azoulay's current inventory search is focused on England, Belgium, France, and Italy. "Experience has made me more discerning but thankfully I'm still not jaded," he says. "I'm always optimistic about my hunt for the next beautiful thing, although there's that silent movie image of a guy walking off one ladder as another shows up and on and on that pretty much sums up my buying process." It also explains why Paolo Ventura's photograph of a man balancing on a high wire dominates the wall facing Azoulay's bed.

As a child he remembers examining tropical fish under microscopes, and as his specimens bred he lined up the tanks in his playroom and mulled over the prospect of becoming a biologist. He held off from collecting anything else until he began working in the menswear

Left: If it weren't for a fifteen-foot-wide alfresco courtyard and a skylit stairwell, each floor of the fifty-foot-long duplex would resemble an enfilade. Polished concrete floors span the length of the hall gallery where Azoulay houses a life-size wooden artist's model fragment, a Sage Vaughn painting, and a Joe Colombo bentwood chair.

Facing page: In a corner of the living room a life-size, articulated wood skeletal figure from the 1880s umpires from an oversize vintage stool. *Low Tide*, a haunting photographic portrait by Robert and Shana ParkeHarrison, hangs above a vintage sofa and one of a pair of bentwood chairs. Azoulay's not sure where he inherited his taste. "My mother grew up in Puerto Rico on a farm and it's hard to categorize her taste more than to say she liked simple, comfortable things," he says. "I don't think I still own anything I grew up with."

fashion industry, and on trips to Southeast Asia and Europe he addictively scouted out new eyewear from Matsuda, Oliver Peoples, and Yohji Yamamoto. Neckties became his next obsession. "I saw them as small, portable pieces of art," he says. Then he expanded into photography, painting, sculpture, objects, and antiques until he'd filled an eighteenth-century Pennsylvania farmhouse to its rafters. A love interest brought him to California, so he packed up a truckload of his possessions, drove it west, and set up shop.

Large, predominantly figurative canvases of magical or fantastical art are the focal point of most rooms. "A friend stayed here recently when I was away and after the first night he checked into a hotel because he was sacred of all the heads and faces," he says. "They have the opposite effect on me. I find them reassuring." He's never motivated to buy art purely because it's blue chip. "Whether something's painted by Damien Hirst or Andy Warhol makes no difference to me whatsoever and I find it pretty tacky when someone describes their art collection by reeling off a list of artists' names. Even more so when they discuss prices they paid."

Similar to his family home, Azoulay's apartment is a necessities-only zone. It's always orderly and clutter-free, and once he carves out a place for an object or canvas it's likely to stay put for years. Apart from Levi, a pony-sized Irish Wolf, he lives alone and has always found the democratic aspect of living with another person challenging. "On my own I'm free to be truly self-expressive without any compromise, without anyone asking me to validate my decisions," he says. "Maybe it's a selfish way of thinking but it extends to the store, where I only sell things I personally covet."

Because he's constantly on the road, there's a commonly held perception that he's a gadfly when in fact he's a confirmed homebody. "I spend as much time as I can here," he says, "because every time I walk in I feel as excited as a kid in a candy store. I have a tremendous affection for my belongings. I feel as if each individual piece is captivating in its own way and that gets amplified when everything's configured together."

Facing page: Azoulay's office contains all the elements of a schoolroom, down to the blackboard. Despite a host of characteristic differences, a Jean Prouvé Compass desk feels akin to a Commes des Garçons bentwood chair, and a melancholic oil painting by Serbian artist Goran Djurovic strongly relates to an unusual, tall male form.

Right: In the dining room three metal-based chairs with adjustable wooden backrests sidle up to an oversize, digitally constructed landscape by the Cuban American photographer Anthony Goicolea. Azoulay grew up sheltered, but felt the whole world open up once he moved to Manhattan. "I feel as if I learned all the things I know now by watching, by observing," he says.

Overleaf: "I rarely sell the things I live with because I'm so attached to them. I can't really explain it, but everything I own has an innocence or honesty that's hard for me to part with," says Azoulay. In the dining room, an oil painting by Goran Djurovic and an Ethan Murrow graphite-on-paper drawing keep company with the taxidermy baboon Azoulay acquired at Deyrolle in Paris.

RENE GONZALEZ

Space, Light, Blurred Edges, and Obscured Delineations

In the guest room of Gonzalez's 900-square-foot apartment a Flexform sofa and Molo paper ottoman are surrounded by a thoughtful group of objects and art. An African loom hangs beneath Rune Stokmo's photographic diptych and Heriberto Mora's symbolic painting of a man in flight. "It was the first work he created after he left Cuba in the early 1990s," says Gonzalez "and I understand friends who get emotional about its symbolism, but I see it as some unearthly landscape." A shelf holds a 1988 Luceplan light, a copper vase Karl Kipp designed in 1906, a shofar Gonzalez bought while in Israel, and a metallic paper collage by a close friend, Cecilia Hernandez.

When Rene Gonzalez explains the thought process behind his architecture it occurs to him that a lot of his theories parallel the work of Robert Irwin, the California light and space artist. For decades Irwin has questioned whether a frame is a necessary containment for his art, and Gonzalez asks the same in the open, unrestricted spaces he designs. Like Gonzalez's buildings, Irwin's installations reevaluate light, blur edges, and obscure delineations. Like Irwin's artwork, Gonzalez's apartments and houses often feature repetitive, rhythmically soothing elements; they leave the difference between in- and outdoors ambiguous and play man-made and innate landscapes against one another.

Gonzalez's projects don't strive to be as meditative as Irwin's. "I'm not creating art. I'm using the language of art and hopefully poetry to create something site specific that meets the needs of my clients," he says. So for an edgy Miami clothing boutique located in a car park sixty feet above Miami Beach he created a glass box whose reflective ceiling and walls act like a movie screen and mirror the street traffic five floors below. For an art exhibition space he transformed a drab eyesore of a warehouse building into an abstracted jungle mural by encrusting its gray facade with a million one-inch-square glass tiles in two hundred shades of yellow and green.

Gonzalez left Cuba when he was three and grew up in South Florida. His family's strong cultural ties to their homeland were evident in the food they ate and the rituals they observed. When he was eight he recalls being glued to his father as he worked on technical diagrams, "and that's what probably inspired me to learn how to draw and then draft," he says. "The connection between spatial arrangements and emotions was apparent to me from an early age, and I used packs of playing cards to lay out floor plans for huge houses with interior courtyards." So it seemed logical for his thesis to debate the psychological impact of space and proportion.

Being close to water felt just as logical, and Gonzalez assumed it was conceivable to trade one ocean or body of water for another so he relocated his studies to UCLA and subsequently spent four years with Richard Meier's firm during the construction of the Getty Center. "In Miami the warmth of the Caribbean seeps into your pores and into every aspect of your daily life, but the Pacific is cold and serves as a barrier when you live in Los Angeles," he says. "So my time on the west coast confirmed my tropical nature, which is why I moved back."

Facing page: A row of shelves in his kitchen is equipped with enough bowls, plates, and containers to cater to an army of guests, even though Gonzalez exclusively eats out. "It's a question of priorities. I'm always on the go and I work day and night," he says. "In fact, my work is my life. But I'm not a workaholic because I love what I do." A container by Massimo and Lella Vignelli epitomizes good design. "Its lid has indentations. They're subtle but graphic indicators that wordlessly tell you to insert two fingers and lift."

Left: In one of two bathrooms, Ivan Kristufek designed a panel out of vintage blue tiles from Czechoslovakia, and the blue resin sink and tray are by Vallvé. Color is often a driving force in Gonzalez's work, particularly in his more public projects like a small hotel in Guatemala, a garden in Saudi Arabia, or a mural in a Toronto pool house. "I always key off of existing, natural colors so I'm reflecting or contrasting the environment. It's fun when I simply turn up the volume on whatever's already there."

As he looks around his South Beach apartment he feels as if he's bursting at the seams. "I think of myself as someone who lives in a very spare way but maybe I need a reality check," he says. "I've never collected any one genre and I'm not interested in name recognition. I like objects where form and function are resolved or where there's an exploration of an idea or intent."

The apartment is bright and looks down onto a shaded garden and an abundance of heliconias, royal palms, and bromeliads. Gonzalez placed a series of scrims against walls and windows to calibrate the various densities of sunlight that filter in throughout the day. The panels also break down thresholds and the traditional demarcations between the various rooms. "Sometimes I think of my apartment as one big canvas, a huge boundary for all the objects it contains," he says. He has a fully equipped kitchen but never cooks, and although its storage cabinets have functioning wheels, like all the art and objects throughout the apartment they stay put. "I never have the desire to rotate things. Things simply have their proper place."

He finds the whiteness of his bedroom to be refreshing and cleansing, and the rest of the apartment extracts its color from the objects and furniture and particularly from the art. "Many of the things I own remind me of a certain moment or a connection I have to a friend, place, or time," he says, "but artwork given to me directly by the artist has a particular resonance because it taps into sense perceptions that are even deeper than conscious memory."

He loves to travel. On a plane with a clear head he's able to pull back, take an overview, and connect the dots and threads in all his projects. "The problem solving automatically happens, I don't have to will it," he says. "Although not when I'm driving, which is why I don't own a car." Being far away from home also opens up his thinking, and the distance gives him creative perspective, as do the seed pods and stones he gathers from different sites he's visited around the world in a way he doesn't fully understand.

Left: Gonzalez purchased the living room's Le Corbusier LC4 pony-hide lounge soon after he graduated from architecture school. He designed the low metal and color-pigmented resin table with Monica Vazquez for a water-themed exhibition, and he acquired the black leather Tobia and Afra Scarpa sofa more than twenty years ago. On the wall, *Blue Shirt* by David Baskin hangs adjacent to two drawings by Venetian artist Walter Michael Pühringer.

Right: A floor-to-ceiling resin divider designed by Gonzalez and Monica Vazquez has flexible edges and divides the kitchen and living room. A photograph of the Florida Everglades by artist Ivan Toth Depeña hangs above a silver version of Marcel Wanders's iconic Knotted chair.

Facing page: A black noodle painting by Robert Melee, a longtime friend, has enormous presence in the master bedroom. "The piece's density changes and dissipates according to the light and the reflections it receives, so it's always in motion," says Gonzalez. Ross Lovegrove's pressed foam Air One chair sits in front of Pollack Studio's hanging Screenery fabric, which conceals a bathroom as well as a neatly organized clothes closet.

On one wall of the master bedroom, beneath a collection of nineteenth-century portrait paintings, a pair of 1920s French chairs with lacquered legs and mother-of-pearl inlay flank a nineteenth-century Venetian gilt and painted marble dragon table. As a child, Willson envisioned himself as an archaeologist, and as a dealer he's heavily focused on the provenance of the objects he acquires. Serrano's historical approach to collecting is lyrically nonmaterialistic and at times finds him carrying stones in his pockets to remind him of traveling pilgrims from past centuries whose sole possessions were a compass and a candle.

ROBERT WILLSON & DAVID SERRANO

Sobriety Keeps the Baroque and Kitsch in Check

When Robert Willson and David Serrano moved in together the prospect of stereophonic collections amassed by two "insatiable buyers" and a shortage of space gave birth to Downtown, their Los Angeles antiques store. "David and I came into this profession late, when we were both in our forties," says Willson, "when we'd accumulated a lotta, lotta stuff." In their decorators' haunt of a shop, design flourishes are frequent and the inventory of debonair vintage classics rotates constantly. In one corner there's a marble console with splayed klismos legs inspired by Arturo Pani alongside a Kelly green Frances Elkins chair, whose back resembles a spindly cluster of carpet beaters, and a pair of Diego Matthai's ladder-back chairs that might be rudimentary if their frames weren't chromed steel. "We're designers more than shopkeepers so our days are spent collaborating with anyone who's in search of something unusual or specific," Willson says. "The items we sell are very much extensions of our personalities."

Similar to the store, their Brookside house, which sits below the Hollywood Hills, is dapper with attainable proportions and an aesthetic core of classic mid-twentieth-century design. The substantive but reductive lines in furniture by Edward Wormley, Gio Ponti, and William Pahlmann provide a foundation for extensive layers of high-voltage accessories and textiles. The simpler pieces ground the exuberance of the more eccentric pieces and provide a sobriety that keeps the baroque and kitsch in stylistic check. "If I didn't know us and I walked in here," says Willson, "I'd guess the inhabitants were curious about life, had some well-kept secrets and a pronounced, slightly wicked sense of humor."

Serrano grew up in Mexicali, Mexico, where the intense light made everything, particularly color, look surreal. "I understand there are people who need to sleep in a calm, neutral bedroom but I'm not one of them," he says. "Just as I need it in my clothing and art I need color to pry my eyes open every morning. I need it to fuel me with a day's worth of energy and passion. It's pure, unadulterated emotion. It triggers the memories of a great afternoon, your lover's eyes, a harmonic piece of music, and anyone who's oblivious to that might just as well live in a monastery."

A happy if belligerent Luddite, Serrano doesn't drive and has no cell phone or iPod, although he occasionally e-mails and regularly follows a blog or two. He dresses like a modern

Left: A 1960s Italian fiberglass chandelier by Sergio Asti hovers over a 1970s Paul Evans burl Parson table and Diego Matthai chairs in the kitchen, which was updated by architect Chip Bohl. "Cooking and decorating are similar," he says, "both processes require measured doses of ingredients but, unlike a dish, a house is never finished. It constantly evolves. It's a living thing."

Facing page: Serrano's extensive, extroverted accessories, including armfuls of ties and leather belts, command a sizable chunk of the master bedroom. The rug is 1960s Moroccan, the Japanese watercolors are nineteenth century, and the hanging textile is 1940s. Surrealism is one of his greatest influences and when he paints and dresses himself he regards colors as gender neutral.

Overleaf: An early-twentieth-century Chinese Coromandel screen adds architectural heft to the dining room, where custom chairs sit around a metal and brass table by Arturo Pani. Artwork includes a framed nineteenth-century Belgian target, a 1960s figurative steel sculpture by Ludvik Durchanek, and a shell bust by Onik Agaronyan. "We always shy away from trends," says Willson. "Trying to be the next best thing is way, way too tiring."

dandy, and close friends draw a blank when they try to recollect him ever wearing an outfit more than once. "I don't care about labels, so it's of no consequence to me if an item was made by Miuccia, Gucci, or Fiorucci," he says. "I have very quiet things in my wardrobe and outrageously loud things." But rather than a peacock Serrano reckons he might have been a crow in a former life. "Why else would I have such a love of collecting feathers, leaves, shells?" Sometimes twigs shaped like letters of the alphabet end up in his collages alongside dead insects.

As a young child Willson kept an orderly scrapbook pasted full of international newspaper front pages at a time when it was customary for headlines to commemorate momentous happenings. He grew up in Ohio, and in the seventh grade he painted his room orange and all its furniture black. "It was awful," he says. "My mother left it that way but she made sure the door remained closed at all times. Even back then I associated personal style with independence, and it taught me a lifelong lesson—if it doesn't work, change it!"

Unlike a lot of people who regularly buy coffee table books, Willson reads most of his from cover to cover, and he and Serrano often spend hours in their living room exchanging ideas. It was the opposite when he was a professional chef and only read the introduction to the cookbooks he bought. "Back then I never read recipes but now I want to learn everything there is to know about design," he says. "It's a thirst. It's part of my worth and appreciation process but I don't see any link between value and money. If I lost everything I own I would simply start again without being incredibly devastated because 90 percent of the fun for me is connected to the research and the hunt, not the capture." Serrano agrees, "I don't relate to pharaohs who were buried with their belongings," he says. "I may suffer when something I own gets broken, but it's temporary. Sentimentality and nostalgia are necessary occasionally but they should never be overused or abused. Things are things and memories are recyclable."

Facing page: A vignette in the living room of the 1938 house includes a nineteenth-century Chinese ribbon altar, a copper Rhinoceros Box by Onik Agaronyan, Line Vautrin mirrors, and a 1917 Henri Ottevaere portrait. "I can't explain it," says Willson, "but things I may not like at first tend to grow into favorites."

Left: Adjacent to the dining area a 1940s cerused oak cabinet designed by Charles Dudouyt anchors an array of ceramics and artwork. A Chinese cloud rug from the 1930s sits beside a nineteenth-century painted leather English chair. "I describe good design," says Serrano, "as my mother sitting in a chair and telling me she's happy and comfortable."

Overleaf: Centered around an Arturo Pani metal and glass table, a 1950s Italian Majolica goat, and Stanislaus Poray's 1950 portrait of Philip G. Benz, a private sitting room to the left of the house's main entrance is a world unto itself. The scenery also contains a 1950s Venetian ceramic Blackamoor floor lamp, Natalie Kruch's Balloona side table, and a 1930s Paul Frankl cement lamp on a Rug Company carpet. "It's an oversimplification to say this about a relationship that's spanned more than a quarter of a century, but as a rule I'm more reserved than David," says Willson. "He's an absolute force but I hold my own. He visualizes things in his head whereas I need to see and touch things. One generalization is true, though—I tend to take things out and he tends to add."

Directly to the right of the apartment's entry, Bricke mated a 1790s marquetry table with a 1982 stainless steel mesh ottoman by Hans Ullrich Bitsch and a Wang Wusheng photograph entitled *Celestial Realm*. The table is topped with a Valdavian stone sculpture from 1580 BC, a Farnese Herakles sculpture that dates back to the mid-first century, and more contemporary objects by Junko Mori and Kondo Takahiro. The bold checkerboard floor defies the dimensions of the small hallway.

RONALD BRICKE

Unlike Beauty, My Memory of Things Ugly Is Short-Lived

From the earliest age Ronald Bricke, who grew up in the Bronx, saw himself as a history buff. When he wasn't tufting his mother's sofas, stripping the veneer off cabinetry, or attempting to build contraptions from the pages of *Popular Mechanics* magazine, he fantasized about early civilizations. On school museum trips his classmates would ogle at dinosaurs while he went off in search of sphinxes. A newspaper clipping from Bricke's senior year at Parsons in Manhattan describes him as a "talented lad" for winning a competition to reimagine the design of a reception hall in the legendary Palladian villa known as La Malcontenta. Two of the judges, the Duchess of Windsor and Salvador Dalí, awarded him the prestigious Pini di San Miniato scholarship in 1961, and the ensuing months of travel and study across Europe enabled him to find a visual voice.

So before he was even financially flush he invested a tidy sum in a bronze, ca. 2000 BC Luristian dagger. "The materiality of ancient objects is exquisite," he says. "No matter whether they're ornate or starkly simple there's always a breathtaking observance of proportion." Born with a strong propensity for beauty, Bricke reckons he's capable of retaining and cataloguing things he considers splendid while he has zero tolerance for anything ugly. "I guess it's discriminatory, but don't ask me to accept a chair as comfortable if it looks unpleasant. I'm not made that way."

At his first position at Yale Burge Interiors, the living spaces he created while assisting Angelo Donghia exuded a quiet glamour and sophistication, but left to his own devices he favored graphic, almost cartoonish color. In a model apartment he checkerboarded a parrot green living room with black and white furniture. The outraged developer simmered down when the unit attracted a string of buyers, and Bricke learned the value and salability of eye-catching drama. Over the years his fluency with color became his calling card, especially when a slew of editorials cited it as his signature, but in reality his clients' tastes always dictate. "If someone is truly stuck on beige, I deliver it," he says. "Otherwise my client wouldn't feel emotionally invested, but I find myself constantly touting color's therapeutic effects."

To prove the point, after he jazzed up the lethally generic architecture of a Tucson tract house with layered shades of pomegranate, turquoise, chartreuse and eggplant, his client's bouts of depression lifted. "The intensity of the southwestern light inspired me to use that palette so it didn't strike me as particularly outlandish," he says. "But there again I can look

Facing page: In the dining area at night, an eighteenth-century Italian silver mirror reflects foliage from the lit terrace as well as the second-century Roman sculpture of Diana and Silenus on the otherwise bare windowsill. The table extends to seat eight people who are served from a tiny adjacent kitchen. Recessed in the lowest portion of the window sits a 1995 Kenzi Misawa rock and steel sculpture.

Left: In the living room a glass vitrine, formerly used in a Milanese department store, corrals the smaller objects and removes any visual clutter from the overall decor. The large Medusa vase is a 1970s work by ceramicist Roy Hamilton. A curved seashell-like form by Siglinda Scarpa occupies a shelf with a fourteenth-to eleventh-century-BC Mycenaean buff-ware chalice above a Valdavian owl sculpture from 1580 BC. The glass sculpture on the lowest shelf is by Dale Chihuly.

Overleaf: Bricke set the sofa on the diagonal to create a larger seating area and designed the floor pattern to drama-tize the room's scale. Two floor-mounted Herakles sculptures and a seated goddess from the first century BC preside over a handsome Klismos chair by T. H. Robsjohn-Gibbings. John Sprouse's artwork from 1990 provides a shock of eye-level color for seated guests; the large graphite drawing is by Frank Boros and the tall nineteenth-century brass urn is by Gustave Serrurier-Bovy.

into the center of a flower and zero in on fifteen different shades." Bricke also calls upon color whenever he needs an instant architectural intervention, like the time he neutralized the enor-mity of a tank-sized Russian red Chesterfield sofa that a client couldn't part with by painting the walls of the room it sat in the same scarlet shade as the upholstery.

In the sharpest of contrasts, the Upper East Side living room he shares with Michael Hill is stark raving white with discreet primary pops. "I literally refuel in its cool fluidity," he says. "It's a sort of 'spring is refreshing after winter' logic. It's how I balance and escape my colorful work life." He tends to choose clients' palettes instinctively, but in his own case he scrolled through more than seventy potential whites, from the coolest to the warmest, and finally settled on a luminous Donald Kaufman shade. By keeping the pristine walls free of art, they function as billboards for the ghostly shadows the room's objects and furniture cast. "The dramatic play of light in here is awesome, and sometimes on a cold, wintry New York day I feel as if I'm sequestered on Santorini or some other Grecian island."

Bricke scatters his Asian ceramics and ancient Roman and Greek artifacts—some dating back to the fourth century BC—across tables and easily within reach where guests can touch and examine them and not feel intimidated by their preciousness. He displays small and particularly fragile bowls, flacons, goblets, urns, and fossils inside a glass showcase to heighten their visual impact. "I don't have a favorite place to sit in here. I alternate from chair to sofa so I get to take in views from every angle," he says. "It's a design fault when someone has to look out onto a horrendous view."

The snowy slipcovers are regularly laundered, so unlike a lot of hosts who fear for the safety of their pristine upholstery Bricke is nonchalant about serving red wine. "In an ideal world a room's decor balances functionality and fantasy, or as Luis Barragán liked to say, the best spaces combine elements of magic, serenity, sorcery, and mystery," he says. "I would add light to that. And of course amusement."

In a small upstairs bedroom the previous owners left behind a portrait of a crinoline-wearing lady, prompting Sharkey to christen it the Marie Antoinette suite. The Victorian wrought iron bed, painted chair, and bamboo screen are all local finds.

RON SHARKEY

Nothing I Buy or Sell Requires White-Glove Handling

Ron Sharkey loosely categorizes the tarnished brass table lamps, mottled stoneware platters, distressed jelly cupboards, faded oil landscapes, and monogrammed linens he picks up at East Coast auctions and estate sales as "Primitive Farmstyle Industrial." But that leaves out their New Victorian, Steampunk, English Shabby, Rough Luxe, and Tractor Chic aspects, and omits the fact that some things he carries are just downright charming.

When he opened his upstate New York store in Accord in 2005 he envisioned it as a glorified garage sale. "I'm fond of the word 'junk,'" he says. "My shingle says 'Antiques' but that's actually too stodgy and pretentious a word for my stuff. Let's just put it this way—nothing I buy or sell requires white-glove handling." On any given Sunday, Hudson Valley locals as well as the occasional boldface Manhattan designer like Brian McCarthy are likely to rub shoulders with regulars like painter Hunt Slonem or photographer John Dugdale as they pick apart Sharkey's artful arrangements, and each customer is likely to refer to the store as his or her personal, off-the-beaten-path secret. "I'm in awe of how many truly talented people shop here, but even though I work closely with a bunch of decorators I don't know how one person can prescribe another person's lifestyle. It's so personal!"

Sharkey caught the "junk" bug early on when, as a child growing up in New Jersey, he accompanied his mother on her regular flea market haunts. "She had a certain way of putting things together," he says. "She once placed heavy chairs around a trestle table. It was a simple gesture but it gave our kitchen an edge. It stopped it from looking suburban." He studied painting, printmaking, ceramics, and photography, and subsequently bartended at night with the intention of making art during the day. Then he took up teaching with a plan to make art during school vacations, but nowadays he channels his creativity into his shop. "When something breaks I never throw it away, and once in a while I work some broken ceramics into a collage, but ideally I should donate all of my shards to a local artist who works in pique assiette."

He crossed over from collector to tradesman once the 1,600-square-foot, 1820s Rondout Creek cottage he bought in 1995 began to resemble a well-fed storage locker and he needed to carve out some living space, but the shop's and house's inventories still shuttle back and forth according to sales or whim. After he won the house in a minor bidding war, it served as his weekend escape from Manhattan for sixteen years and once he moved in full time he

Left: A line of stoneware pitchers decorates the top of a painted closet under an 1840s portrait of a bull on the upstairs landing. "When I buy I'm very decisive, but if I grow tired of something I'd rather sell it for less than my buying price," says Sharkey. "I like objects to move in and out of my life. My main regrets are the ones I let slip through my fingers."

Facing page: In the kitchen/dining room a high wall shelf displays ironstone platters, a corner cabinet holds more stoneware, and a wooden hay rake leans against the wall. Sharkey frequently rotates the furniture in this room, depending on the size of the store's inventory, and at one point he had a long table that sat twelve. "The concept was great," he says, "but in reality I never need to seat more than four people here. In a small house you can't have too many chairs because they double up as side tables and they're easy to move around." French doors lead to a screened-in porch on one side and the garden on another. A cast iron, wood-burning stove warms the entire house on cool days.

landscaped its two-acres with boxwood hedges and plump hydrangea bushes. "I feel blessed to be its current caretaker," he says. "It's secluded so it attracts curiosity and occasionally I find myself playing tour guide. Afterwards people tell me they feel as if they've just temporarily been transported out of current day America!"

As evidenced by a residue of staple marks, Sharkey's bedroom floor was formerly protected with a drop cloth while the room functioned as a painting studio. "I inherited its wallpaper," he says. "I wouldn't have had the nerve to put it up myself and I didn't have the heart to take it down. Actually, in a weird way, all along all the rooms dictated their needs to me and I complied. I thought about mixing in some contemporary pieces but the rooms didn't want that." Patina, evidence of use, and spirit over status are distinguishing characteristics of Sharkey's stock. "I'm not big on the provenance of things. I'm not all that concerned about where things came from or who owned them. That feels like the past. I'm very matter of fact, very 'it is what it is.'" Some dealers wouldn't dream of interfering with an object's authenticity, but Sharkey feels the opposite, so although he loves tattered originals he often reupholsters sofas, seats, and armchairs. "When I notice a repair or a restoration I know someone valued something enough to breathe new life into it, and that fact alone connects me emotionally. Occasionally I go through a phase where I don't want anything chipped and cracked but that generally lasts for about ten seconds."

He's always had a preference for muted, faded colors, apart from a blip when he painted his fraternity dorm room tomato red around the same time he acquired a cone-shaped black metal lantern. "It was missing a piece of glass and its handle was slightly imperfect but it had good, strong lines and overall it had a nice crustiness. It never rusted so I've never needed to paint it or even clean it and at this point I've owned it for forty-five years! I'll never sell it," he says. "But I guess I should never say never!"

Facing page: The open staircase particularly impressed Sharkey when he first viewed the house. "It's as steep as a ladder, and there's something charming and odd about that," he says. "It tells me that the house wasn't a rote building job. Like us all, it has its eccentricities." He left the original chipped linoleum as is and viewed each tread as a display opportunity. The structure now fulfills the role of a stepped shelf unit, holding stacks of books, a glass jar full of turkey feathers he's found in the garden, and some curvaceous ceramics.

Left: The living room wallpaper also came with the house. A pile of New York City tree bark he displays under a glass specimen dome sits next to a taxidermy bird and a painted tin lamp. Sharkey grew up with the oil painting. "I guess it has a lot of sentimental value because my father bought it from a merchant marine," he says. "I believe it's Dutch."

Right: In a spare room is one of a pair of demilune tables Sharkey bought for a song at a yard sale; the other items—a mortar and pestle, a stack of leather-bound books, and a still life of rhododendrons—came from auction or from local dealers. "I overlook chips and tears," he says. "They're the equivalent of human wrinkles."

Overleaf: The cross-ventilated master bedroom looks out directly onto the creek and is a well-ordered repository for a host of flea market and auction finds. "The absence of people, and the mountains, river, and sky I see from here are a perfect antidote to the bustle of the shop, and at the same time I'm emotionally invested in all my belongings," says Sharkey. He has no television, but he often watches movies on his computer. "I'm a homebody, particularly in the winter, so rustic life, where you have to submit to the seasons, suits me."

Campbell sometimes fantasizes about moving back to the West Coast and living in a Case Study house or an Arts and Crafts–style house designed by Julia Morgan, "But maybe not full time," he says. "I've become such a New Yorker." Particular things he loves on the living room wall facing the windows include a watercolor by Steven Mueller; a piece by his friend, the artist Keith Sonnier, called a *Holocene Shelf*; and a found drawing by Keith Haring from 1984. The portrait of Andy Warhol dressed in drag is by Christopher Makos, and there's an invitation/announcement signed by Warhol from the show he did with Jean-Michel Basquiat at Tony Shafrazi in 1985. A library wall of shelves, situated behind a Heywood Wakefield Wishbone table, holds stacks of books Campbell has yet to read.

SCOTT CAMPBELL

The Sky and a Harmonious, Controlled Piece of Chaos

When Scott Campbell sits or lounges on his living room sofa he looks out onto a broad expanse of sky above downtown Manhattan or a wall of floor-to-ceiling bookshelves or a thirty-year-old assemblage of photographs, collages, prints, and paintings that wallpaper the room's remaining two sides. Each perspective strikes Campbell as contemplative and soothing. "It's very balanced," he says. "In one direction I'm meditating on nature and in the other I have harmonious chaos. Under any circumstances life in New York is full of hectic drama, and here inside my little apartment I have a manageable piece of the pie alongside its antidote."

The art extends into the hallway, bedroom, kitchen, and bathroom, and as its salon-style arrangement considers every inch of wall space to be prime real estate, the 800-square-foot space feels surprisingly large. Some of the depictions are heartfelt; some are edgy. A pastoral grouping wouldn't feel out of place at a hushed vernissage, while a neighboring row of edgy portraits is straight out of a cocktail party. Nothing is hung according to subject matter, medium, time period, color, or size, and yet the diversity of visual statements feels integrated. And because each individual work refers to an aspect of Campbell's life in its entirety, it's a reassuring testimony to the complexity of the human spirit.

Campbell grew up in Northern California in an agricultural region known for its vineyards and pear orchards, and he spent much of his childhood out of doors swimming in the ocean every summer and skiing every winter. He read about communities of water colorists who chronicled the western landscape in the 1960s and 1970s and felt an affinity with artists like Emile Norman who made no distinction between their life and art. He attended UC Berkeley, where studying art history changed his life, and he still owns a commemorative photograph from the period, Richard Misrach's painterly study of the Golden Gate Bridge, which happens to be his first gallery acquisition. "It's hilariously sentimental," says Campbell, "and after all this time I still appreciate it. By nature I'm not the remotest bit nostalgic. It may not be apparent but I don't live in the past. I'm much more excited about the future."

Before he'd set foot in New York, Campbell knew the city well from watching Woody Allen movies like *Manhattan* and *Annie Hall* a zillion times, plus he'd followed Andy Warhol's antics and so was also enamored with the city's wilder, raunchier side. When he came east he planned to find work in noncommercial theater, but the HIV epidemic took precedence. An

Left: In the bedroom a work by David Hilliard hangs alongside Ron Church's photograph of two surfers, above Jeff Divine's photograph of surfers in the water off the coast of Santa Barbara. Just before she died in 2010, the artist Louise Bourgeois created the depiction of two red flowers joined to a single stem, entitled *I Do*, for the organization Freedom to Marry.

Facing page, clockwise from top left: Campbell's home office occupies a corner of his bedroom where two David Armstrong photographs—a portrait and a nighttime shot of Times Square—face each other.

The triptych photograph above the bed, entitled *Jesus in the Waiting Room*, is by David Hilliard, and the nude was a gift from photographer John Scott. A framed needlepoint embroidery sewn by Campbell's grandmother hangs above a few pieces he picked up at antiques shops in the East Village during the mid-1980s. "The photograph of me dates back to 1985," he says. "It was taken on the Lower East Side by a dear friend, Pablo Prietto, and it brings back a lot of memories."

A large piece by Barney Kulok occupies one wall of the hallway above a George Nelson bench. On the wall leading into the living room, a painting by the German artist Matthias Reinmuth and a photograph by the artist Jack Pierson occupy the top row above two paintings by Matthew Brandt.

involvement with the American Foundation for AIDS Research and the infuence of its founding chairwoman, Mathilde Krim, who remains a friend, eventually led him to the Elton John AIDS Foundation, where he is currently executive director. "The eighties was a seminal period for me. I loved my life in New York—the good and the bad. It was a very extreme time," he says. "We were racing against the clock to fund a cure for HIV, so every moment was adrenaline charged. Every moment counted and we didn't take anything and anyone for granted."

Christopher Makos's photographic interpretation of Warhol in the semi-drag guise of his feminine persona Lady Warhol now lords over the living room, and along with every other photograph, painting, and sculpture, Campbell recalls exactly when it was acquired. Many pieces came directly from friends or from winning bids he placed at charity auctions. "It's great to support artists and a cause you believe in at one and the same time," he says. Due to the sheer volume of his holdings, people often refer to Campbell as a collector, but he finds the term to be pompous and he balks at its aloof, professional connotation. "I only buy work when I have a high regard for the artist or subject matter, so if a collector is someone who's devoted to art and looks to it for refuge then I guess I qualify. I don't confine creativity to an artistic endeavor. I see it harnessed in a multitude of different ways. I see it evidenced in doctors, nurses, and many of the people I deal with every day. So art in all its many forms is a very personal part of my life. It's not just what I put on my walls."

Overleaf: The longest wall of the living room is also plastered with art and includes a favorite painting by the artist James Brown, a Steven Meisel portrait of Liza Minnelli, and a Todd Selby photograph entitled *Karl in His Library*. The black on black print on the wall's right edge, an edition called *My Fear Is Your Fear*, was created by Glenn Ligon for an AIDS organization close to twenty years ago. Campbell bought the rug during a trip to Buenos Aires, and he asked for assistance from a friend, interior designer Rob Southern, before he reupholstered the twenty-year-old sofa. Southern insisted on preserving the pair of scruffily upholstered Eames chairs.

SHAMIR SHAH & MALCOLM HILL

Shoot Me If My Designs Ever Reek of Ostentation

Shamir Shah's suburban family house sat in close proximity to verdant tea plantations and a national park where prides of wild lions roamed freely. A short drive away, in Nairobi, a formal plan of classical and beaux-arts-influenced buildings dominated the city's center. When Shah eventually studied architecture at Yale, he got his first taste of culture shock. "I'd traveled to Europe a lot but New Haven was my first experience of the States," he says, "and I'd imagined the campus as a series of heroic buildings set into a pastoral landscape. I never dreamt it would be all chain link fences and urban grit." These days Shah is such a confirmed metropolitan he takes his life in his hands every day to bicycle the thirty-block distance between his mid-Manhattan loft and SoHo studio.

Design consistently intrigued Shah throughout his childhood. In his early teens he had the opportunity to study the blueprints and witness the construction of his uncle's sprawling Mediterranean-style house, and he was riveted. Then there was the appealing way an aunt combined English antiques with contemporary chairs and African tribal artifacts in her Colonial farmhouse. "I remember asking her to logically explain why things from such wildly different cultures blended together so well. I understood it visually but couldn't get it rationally," he says. In his grandmother's house, where monkeys cavorted along the branches of mango trees in an inner courtyard, all the structural materials catered to the climate and kept rooms cool on warm days. "These places from my childhood all had soul, a kind of harmony I'd like to say I incorporate into the projects I design today."

A few years ago, when Shah completed the architectural conversion of a 1930s warehouse in Chelsea, he and his partner, Malcolm Hill, decided to leave their small Greenwich Village apartment and move into one of its open lofts. Hill, a painter and sculptor, grew up in Texas and when he bought his first house at age twenty-six he turned it into an art installation by loosely covering its walls with large sheets of paper that he had inscribed with poetry. "I was deeply bohemian at the time and was rather scathing about fancy-pants style. I wanted my living environment to be all about expression," says Hill. "I still do to a certain degree, which is why I provide the art here, but it's clearly in both of our interests for Shamir to take charge of the furnishings."

Left: Shane Ruth's balsa-wood bull's head is mounted adjacent to the open kitchen, where shelves display white china and glassware.

Facing page: Hill builds most of his larger paintings and sculptures in his Montana studio, where he has plenty of solitude and space. His bas-relief wall piece in plaster, found wood, and linen canvas dominates one wall of the living space close to a Poul Kjærholm leather chair and an assemblage of travel mementos. "The longer Shamir and I are together," he says, "the more our color choices and palettes merge and pare down, and there's something wonderfully reassuring about that. It's as if we're singing the same tune."

Travel mementos cover most of the loft's surfaces. Shah points to a red and white beaded Karnataka bracelet they bought from a woman who was selling wares on a beach in Southern India just after Hill was stung by jellyfish. Next to it is an ebony stick he picked up off the ground of the Serengeti and a dried piece of seaweed he found washed up on the beachfront near a house they formerly owned on Fire Island. "Once in a while a client asks me for a turn-key project where I would supply every piece of their personal minutiae, but I can't do it," he says. "Decorating up to the gills for someone besides Malcolm strikes me as way too personal and intrusive. I collaborate heavily with my clients to create a home that feels totally relevant but I stop short at providing the evidence of their inner life. "

The loft's structural simplicity shows how opposed Hill and Shah are to tricked-out architecture. "I'm not a fan of bathrooms where chandeliers double as showerheads; where aromatherapy vaporizes out of the walls," says Shah. "Give me heated floors, noiseless air conditioning, plenty of wall space for art, drawers that glide easily, and doors that close silently. True luxury is all of those invisible, behind-the-scenes things. Shoot me if ever I design anything that reeks of ostentation."

Along the way many architects influenced and shaped Shah's aesthetic. There's Louis Kahn, who manipulated light so masterfully; Rudolph Schindler, who infused unapologetically modern design with warmth and humanity; Richard Neutra, who achieved a seamlessness between indoor and outdoor living; and Geoffrey Bawa, who incorporated indigenous Sri Lankan crafts into his quietly solid buildings. "I'm still drawn to things that remind me of my heritage, and I wish I owned two remnants from my childhood," says Shah. The first is a portrait his father painted of a majestic tawny owl, and the second is a massive mahogany wardrobe his grandmother kept in her bedroom. Behind doors covered with hand-painted scrolls and motifs she kept boxes of candy and neat piles of folded saris. "My dad's painting is long gone, and periodically I look out for Indian antiques, but so far nothing similar to that armoire seems to have strayed into my life."

Facing page: In the den Shah framed a collection of his life drawings and hung them on a wall of bark cloth alongside vintage family portraits and photographs he's taken while traveling. "I am very close to my family," says Shah. "I have lots of relatives in Kenya and I visit them regularly. Even though I consider myself to be a New Yorker I still identify with my birthplace."

Below: In one part of the open loft the dining area doubles as a library space and one wall of shelves holds well used art books. The stained oak dining table and walnut and leather bench are by SS Design, the chandelier is by David Weeks, the bronze candlesticks are early-twentieth-century Japanese, and the framed photograph of a Las Vegas land-scape is by Ofer Wolberger. "Nature is enormously important to me," says Shah, who at one point wanted to be a vet, "but in general, I'm drawn toward authen-ticity in whatever form that appears. Kitsch and appliquéd are of little appeal."

Above: Two sofas—one designed by Shah; the other a vintage Jens Risom—occupy a corner of the loft close to a David Weeks lamp and Ty Best's oak side table, where a macramé sculpture by Mary Haslip hangs above artwork by Hill and Brett Windham. "As I grew up in Africa," says Shah, "I have an instinctive or uncon-scious feel for that culture and aesthetic. I have no line of connection to European antiques so they're not really a part of my visual vocabulary. However, I could easily live in Russel Wright's Manitoga, where all your activities are an inch away from nature."

An unattributed 1925 French glass-fronted cabinet occupies a wall in the large living area and reflects a sitting room beyond; above it is one of Justin Beal's rubber paintings. The low stacks of antique art books belonged to Lavin's grandfather, and the mounted lozenge, from the 1960s, is by Terry O'Shea. "I'm attracted to furniture, art, and design that has some kind of vision and cohesion. I like things that are layered, but I also love things that are pithy and reductive," says Lavin. "Anything that's overtly one track, whether it's traditional, antique, or contemporary, feels pedantic. I also don't need for my things to be all that utilitarian. I'd prefer them to make some kind of visual or theoretical statement."

THOMAS LAVIN

In a Disciplined Glass House, Where Would I Hang My Art?

Thomas Lavin intimately recollects the Pacific Palisades ranch his grandfather, Richard Irvine, a senior figure at Walt Disney, built in 1952. As a child he totally appreciated its exquisite quality, lavish scale, grand formality, and luxurious colors. Irvine flew an artist in from Japan to execute an Oriental scene on the entry room's walls; family dinners for fourteen centered around an enormous table; and in the living room a palette of celadon and salmon pink flattered an abundance of "good enough" antiques—nineteenth-century reproductions of eighteenth-century originals. The house and grounds contained the wondrous and scary elements of a classic fairy tale. "All the rooms overlooked an expansive lawn, and my grandmother cordoned off her formal rose garden behind a white fence," he says, "and I knew sure death awaited me if I strayed beyond that boundary!"

Collecting boxes—stylistically random, from pill to glove size, filled with buttons, letters, and drawings—was one of his first attempts at establishing privacy, but it was pretty short-lived once his brother learned how to pick locks. From the earliest age he saw fashion as a means of creative expression, and he still treasures a South American doll his grandmother gave him when he was four—he even made a contemporary version of its native outfit when the original grew threadbare. By college age he began thinking in more expansive, theatrical terms, and it felt natural for him to festoon his dorm walls with vintage Yves Saint Laurent capes, luscious kimonos, hats, and shirts. "In the end, those overly romantic years of excess and indulgence brought home the importance of brutal editing. They taught me to isolate an object so its essence shines out," he says. "That's also when I realized how restored I felt whenever I was exposed to tranquilizing colors. And once I was introduced to beige I learned to see depth and beauty in the negation of color."

Lavin left UCLA with a bachelor's degree in art history, and after a few years as an event planner he managed to-the-trade showrooms until he eventually opened his own at the Pacific Design Center, where he now represents furniture, lighting, textiles, and accessories from sixty different designers. He interacts with people all day, so he chose to live on a property in Santa Monica where the house is cordoned off from the street by a small courtyard and garden, and its interior, which interior designer Gary Hutton reconfigured, has private and public aspects. "I have distinct options. I can comfortably entertain two hundred people in the very

Left: In a corner of the open dining area, Madeline Stuart chairs sit beneath a nineteenth-century candelabrum Lavin inherited from his grandparents, which Gary Hutton mounted onto a minimal steel bracket. Lavin grew up in an orderly home. "It wasn't formal but we had rules," he remembers. "Punctuality was key and we were allowed in the living room to play Scrabble, but otherwise it was reserved for guests."

Facing page: In a side sitting room a sculptural Gary Hutton banquette sits at right angles to a naturally formed teakwood-root table beneath a pair of hand scored Joe Goode lithographs from the 1970s. Lavin decorated the house using the same philosophy he applies to his showroom, where his eye and his gut guide him. "Every piece has to relate to its neighbor as well as the broader context," he says, "so it's a question of nit-picking the details and taking a macro view at one and the same time. I guess that pretty much sums up the way I approach my life in general."

large living room or I can be solitary in the master suite or den, which is the nearest thing I'll ever get to a man cave," he says. "I like austere architecture, so something built by John Pawson would also suit me well, or I could be happy in a privately sited version of Philip Johnson's Glass House. But then where would I hang all my art?"

Lavin's collection of paintings comes from a group of emerging and established Los Angeles artists. "I avoid vivid color," he says, "and I respond well to graphic, masculine work where the maker's hand shows in the brush strokes or tracks of paint." Travel counts as a major source of inspiration, and he defies anyone to be jaded once they're fully immersed in another culture. His sense of equilibrium is rooted in order; he likes his objects to stay in their assigned areas and hangs his shirts according to their color and sleeve length. "I think of my style as contemporary dandy. I'm always trying to pare things back but I never succeed. I guess I don't really know how. Dressing is costume, it's play, and no matter what we put on we're always assuming a character. I get excited every time I dress."

Lavin used to sport slim-lined, tailored suits and bold ties until he realized the uniform thwarted his creativity, and these days on an average weekend his getup is likely to look extreme—black satin culotte leggings, combat boots, patent leather bag, and a burgundy hide-on-hide sweater. "In public places people tend to stop and stare," he says, "but I don't pay attention anymore. Fashionwise I think it would be fantastic to go back to Edwardian England or to court life at Versailles or during Louis XVI's reign but not later than 1790."

He currently collects few things and wears rather than displays his favorite outfits, but he's returned to his early love of containers and is particularly fond of the Japanese craft perfected by the Samurai, who were forced out of sword making and directed their skills to creating steel boxes with gold and enamel overlays. "I guess there's something comforting about getting back to where it all started."

Left: Lavin's shoe inventory includes well-worn leather slip-ons and Duckie Brown's dapper bronze-leaf lace-ups. His well-appointed wardrobe currently contains labels by several Dutch designers as well as Alexander McQueen, Jil Sander, Lanvin, and Prada.

Below: The assortment of artwork, including pieces by Brian Sharp, casually leans and hangs in the den. "I was a piano major at UCLA," he says, "so I love classical music. But I'm more attracted to mood than a particular genre. Aaron Copland at the Walt Disney Concert Hall is genius because the theatre is built to accommodate the grandeur of his compositions. I also like intimate chamber ensembles, and I regularly have season subscriptions to the Los Angeles Philharmonic. When I travel I always scope out local theatre and music happenings."

Facing page: In the extremely tailored master suite a custom bed by Antoine Proulx sits on a silk Gary Hutton rug. Lavin reads here a lot. "Mainly biographies, every book I can find about Mary, Queen of Scots, and I love Antonia Fraser—I eat up her books. I'm intermittently obsessed with the Mitford Sisters, and I went through a Truman Capote phase, but then I also read business books and things written by Malcolm Gladwell."

Overleaf: In the main living room a pair of Gary Hutton chairs flanks an elegant sofa by William Haines. A pair of cockatoo lamps Lavin acquired from his grandparents sit on mismatched 1940s Swedish chests, and the painting is by Allison Miller. Miniature boxes dot available flat surfaces and Lavin is often surprised at their contents. "There's usually some kind of rediscovery," he says, "a process of reattaching to something I've stored away and forgotten about."

Immediately inside the house, a shadow box of hand-forged metal implements—from door hooks to spatulas and keys—sits on a functioning radiator. In front of massive moose and elk antlers, a glass-fronted cabinet stores a family of clothed dolls and porcelain heads that Pfeffer began accumulating when he was in college. "I guess there's a fair amount of stigma attached to collecting dolls," he says, "which is probably why my daughters have incorporated them into their artwork. Maybe that's also why I've placed them in a highly visible place, so they're the first thing people comment on when they enter the house."

TOM PFEFFER

Collecting's Not About the Money, It's About the Mission

Twenty years ago Tom Pfeffer moved his family from Brooklyn to the Hudson Valley in order to rescue a beautiful, late-eighteenth-century house that sits in the middle of Kingston, footsteps away from one of the city's busiest streets. Unbeknownst to most passersby, the house backs onto ten bucolic acres of sweeping landscape, a former flood plane where eighty-year-old willows and century-old maple trees preside over a bird-feeding retreat. Pfeffer currently tends hives of bees, and over the years he's kept ducks, chickens, and at least three baby sheep who made front-page headlines in the local newspaper when they wandered off the property and strolled uptown. Steeped in history, the house was badly burned by the British in 1773, and many of its early features—fireplace surrounds and staircases—are long gone, but its original limestone facade is still intact.

The house ranks as Pfeffer's third reclamation project, and he links his drive to save abandoned or unloved properties to his liberal upbringing. "Rescuing anything that's been left for dead is life-affirming and creative in the most fundamental way," he says. No doubt his mother, who refinished and reupholstered the antiques she picked up for a song and placed in their rambling family home, influenced him. "The yard sales she took me to definitely turned me into a hunter-gatherer." Current collections include animal skulls, prison shivs, birds' nests, carved walking sticks, flax combs, porcelain dolls, and metal choppers. When a tortoise shell fractures into a handful of pieces or when a ceramic vase cracks, Pfeffer treats it as if it's a jigsaw puzzle and painstakingly glues it all back together.

He's seduced by the obsolete, by items technology has usurped or by tools people deride as "old-fashioned," and he avoids buying anything bright and garish so no one thing upstages its neighbor when it's on display. His "strength in numbers" principle involves him ganging up multiples of a kind—turned wooden bowls, handheld cameras—so their en masse presence serves as a room's architectural focal point. He enjoys the hunt more than the actual acquisition, so when he's keen on an item and finds its status elevated to a hot collectible he backs off. "I'll always love yellow ware bowls but I stopped buying them when they became pricey. It's not about the money, it's about the mission."

Two of his most prized possessions formerly belonged to his mother. A nineteenth-century framed Audubon print of a green heron and an oak Stickley armchair that's still as

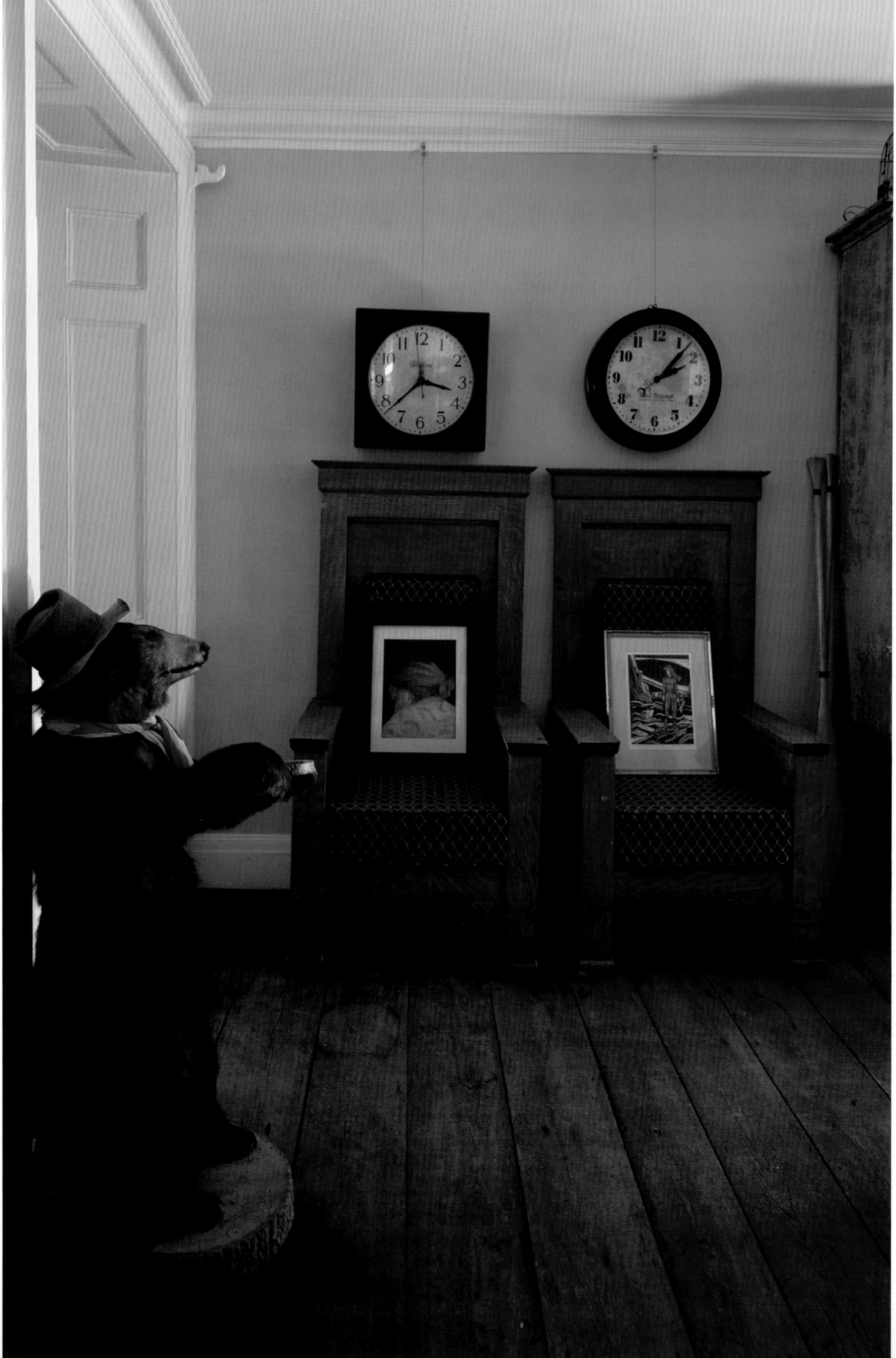

Facing page: In the dining room two clocks crown a pair of high-backed oak Masonic temple chairs. Eric Angeloch created the oil painting, and Carol Zaloom created the linoleum cut—they're both portraits of Pfeffer's partner, Susan Hereth. He acquired the taxidermy bear from an upstate New York flea market. The wide-planked floors are original to the house.

Right: Pfeffer found the ten-foot-long late-1800s oak and pine table in an abandoned building in Manhattan, and he stripped the early 1900s kitchen cabinet down to its weathered undercoat. He bought the bronze flower from Lowell Nesbitt's estate more than twenty years ago and picked up the African bead and shell hanging in a flea market.

sturdy as it was when it was constructed in the early 1900s. Pfeffer's children often refer to the attic as a branch of the Goodwill, and they're used to serendipitous finds like the bevy of flannel shirts their father wore in college, a twenty-foot-long snake's skin, or a horde of orphaned chairs. "When they were growing up, I made a point to emphasize how effortless it is to spend a hundred dollars on a bottle of wine," he says, "but how challenging it is to find a good bottle of wine for ten dollars, and I think they're more enterprising as a result."

Some arrangements feel composed while others feel like spontaneous bricolage. "I place things intuitively and hope the end result allows the individual attributes—the materiality, texture, or shape, of each piece—to come across, and I often channel Andy Goldsworthy," he says, referring to his favorite artist, who creates lyrical assemblages by scavenging rocks, lichen twigs, and pods from the fields and streams around his house in Scotland. Like Goldsworthy, Pfeffer is an environmentalist, and he and his partner, Susan Hereth, own a small 1950s cabin in the Adirondacks. "It's just large enough for us to sleep and make coffee in. A base for us to hike, swim, canoe, and forage."

One of his favorite books is Henry Beston's *The Outermost House*. Written in 1928, it poetically documents a naturalist's life over the course of a year as he lives in a beach cottage on the dunes of Cape Cod. "I have my sights set on a 1955 aluminum Spartan trailer home," he says, "and I fantasize about living there with my two dogs." Sometimes he thinks it could be fun to own a sleek modern house and very few belongings but he enjoys his bouts of sentimentality and can't imagine forsaking the pleasure he derives from stewarding all of his possessions. "I was once on a cross-country bicycle trip with everything I needed packed into a couple of saddlebags and I was surprised to find that freedom of existence so intoxicating. At one point in California my bags got stolen and I wasn't the least bit devastated."

Above: Pfeffer was intimidated by the photos the real estate agent first showed him of the neglected house because he knew his restoration plans didn't involve him furnishing it in period. "I had no desire to fill it with Chippendale," he recalls, "and I asked myself whether that was disrespectful or not."

Left: The little structure Pfeffer built on the house's expansive property to house sheep, chickens, and beehives looks and feels as if it's located in deep seclusion.

Facing page: In one of two front parlors Pfeffer installed a primitive breakfront, topped it with an assortment of baskets and paper wasps' nests, then rapidly filled its interior with pottery and wood bowls. Polished lingams take up floor space while a Halloween mask occupies the Irish famine chair Pfeffer inherited from his mother when he was twenty-five.

Left: In front of a ground-floor window, Pfeffer's favorite skull, that of a horse, sits on top of a stack of boxes above a row of hand-carved wood numbers. "I found it buried in an old stone wall," he says, "and I swear it's smiling."

Below: In a spacious guest bedroom, Pfeffer assigned a glass cabinet to hold a wide range of turned wood bowls. He "splurged" for the hippo skull while he was traveling in Alaska. "I tend to run in the opposite direction of trends," he says. "I'm not drawn to things other people covet."

Facing page: Pfeffer's vast camera collection dates back to the 1950s and takes up most of the landing on the back hall stairs alongside a graphic display of rubber laboratory gloves.

Overleaf: In the family room, shelves on either side of a bar back mirror hold rows of girlie glasses from the 1950s, surrounding a reflection of a Tom Ferris painting that hangs above an opposite mantel. Pfeffer has hundreds of bowls of every size and material, and he has a particular fondness for yellow ware. "I would be hard pressed," he says, "to name anything I own that's brand new."

232

Plastering the walls of the entry hall, Frank Thiel's 1994–98 photographic series, entitled *The Allies*, is by far the most dramatic installation in the villa. It's an eerie commemoration of some of the French, Russian, British, and American soldiers who occupied West Berlin during the cold war. The industrial table and chairs, from the 1940s, are by the celebrated French metal worker Raymond Subes, and the strip lighting originated in a 1920s Berlin casino.

WOLFGANG JOOP

Sometimes I Feel As If I Need an Invitation to My Own Life

For the last decade Wolfgang Joop has lived in what he calls "splendid isolation" in his hometown of Potsdam, less than twenty miles from the center of Berlin, in a 20,000-square-foot villa built in 1908 as an embassy. He rarely goes into town and the commute to his studio, where he heads his Joop! fashion label, is a short hundred-yard sprint away in an equally massive late-nineteenth-century red brick mansion. "Yes, I inhabit a strange planet," he says. "Sometimes I feel as if I need an invitation to my own life!"

Journalists fastidiously document the comings and goings of his career and quote his succinct comments about the state of the industry. "Hemlines and headlines! The fashion world is a battlefield but it has a tremendously intimate side," he says. "After all, the things I create become a woman's second skin." His adjunct careers as an actor, magazine editor, illustrator, and journalist garner less press, although several international galleries sell his sculpture and paintings, in which angels are a recurring theme. "I was a lonely child and I related to the ones I saw clustered around cemetery graves. They always looked peaceful," he says. "I imagined them as messengers and guides from another realm. I never put people in my art because I deal with the human form all day."

As a child in postwar East Germany, Joop had the run of Sanssouci, Frederick the Great's eighteenth-century summer palace. A short walk away from his grandparents' home and open to the public, its lax security enabled him to play in its terraced gardens. He interviewed imaginary princesses from previous centuries in its whimsical Rococo salons and pressed his nose up against its opulent oil paintings. "We were poor so I had no toys but I perceived that as an advantage because it meant the world was my playground and Sanssouci was a parallel dimension, a real-life fairy tale. I felt super rich. Maybe that's why I am so perverse," he says. "You can only know beauty if you experience ugliness, and you can only recognize luck if you taste misfortune."

Once Joop took ownership of the former embassy, he christened it Villa Wunderkind and commissioned the esteemed late architect Josef Paul Kleihues to shore up an Italian Neoclassical facade and radically change its interior by converting its main floor into lofty rooms with museum proportions. The converted three-story space now has few doors, and its white walls are fitting backdrops for any and all of the periods of art in Joop's sizable inventory.

Facing page: An oil portrait by the eighteenth-century Swedish court painter Carl Frederik van Breda hangs above a 1955 Folke Jansson sofa. Joop tends to intermittently purge his inventory of design and art, and several years ago he sold a collection of ten Tamara de Lempicka paintings spanning a twenty-five year period. "Tamara is my soul mate," he says. "It was love at first sight and we lived together for a long time, but the relationship came to an end and I was able to let them go without a shred of nostalgia."

Left: On Joop's property a steel version of *Angel of the North* by the British sculptor Antony Gormley orients toward the Heiligensee, across from the marble palace of the Prussian King Friedrich Wilhelm II. When Joop opens his windows he hears the sound of crows, jackdaws, and church bells.

As a child he gathered caterpillars and butterflies and wondered at their metamorphosis, and as an adult with an unrestricted budget he filled the villa with a twenty-year-old collection of decorative arts from the 1930s and 1940s, and freely mixed in old master paintings and contemporary art. "I have prime examples of Gothic, Bauhaus, Art Deco, Biedermier, and Art Nouveau, and it all fits together but not in an obvious way," he says. "I'm drawn to craftsmanship, excellent materials, and rarity, and I like things that deal with conflict in some way. Here a mix of classical beauty and irritation, there a mix of respect and disrespect. At the end of the day I'm attracted to objects and people for the same reason—for their originality and character."

He's never cared about literal comfort, and his furniture configurations don't particularly take convenience and social interactions into consideration. "That's just not the way I think," he says. "I'm incapable of creating cozy situations." Villa Wunderkind is oriented toward Heiligensee, which translates as "the sacred lake," and Joop feels calmed by the constant smell of its aromatic, brackish froth while close-by buildings ooze historical importance. There's the site where Stalin and Churchill signed treaties; the sound stage where Fritz Lang and Marlene Dietrich made classic movies; the nearby Glienicke Bridge, where Russia traded captured spies during the cold war and in the pages of John Le Carre's novels. "I have lots of terraces and balconies and each one of my views is more surreal than the next," he says. "I can see castles and huge expanses of sea and sky and sometimes such idyllic beauty feels totally oppressive. And then I'm as overwhelmed as the main character in Lars von Trier's movie *Melancholia*." Whenever those moods descend he comes home, rushes past the art and furniture, goes upstairs to his bedroom with his dogs—Charlotte, a Rhodesian Ridgeback, and Gretchen, a Dalmatian—and slams the door shut. "Then, at other times, when I realize no one owns beauty because it's simply not for sale, I can be in awe of the sunsets here and I feel as if I should be on my knees."

Facing page: The dining room is a highly ornate counterpart to some of the starker rooms. During the day light floods in, but at nighttime a 1900s chandelier attributed to Koloman Moser and a pair of Louis XV tree branch sconces from the mid-eighteenth-century are its main sources of illumination. The German five-paneled screen is eighteenth-century, the gilt wood open armchairs are Louis XVI, the 1930s wrought iron dining table is by Gilbert Poillerat, the matched set of silvered side chairs are Italian, and the mirror is Prussian Rococo.

Below: A mid-eighteenth-century gilt mirror from southern Germany sits above a silvered console from the same period opposite a two-part cherub and skull sculpture by the Scottish artist Kenny Hunter.

Above: Joop's 2004 sculpture entitled *Birds Can Fly* is stationed facing the villa's entrance. "I'm at peace with angels," he says. "It's why I keep coming back to them in my art."

Overleaf, left: Gretchen, Joop's pet dalmatian, curls up in a mid-1940s Jean Royère armchair. In the background is a gold-lacquered side cabinet Jean Dunand originally designed for the French milliner Madame Agnés in 1926 and a hand-carved wood totem by Alexandre Noll sits beneath a seventeenth-century still life painted by Simon Pietersz Verelst. Joop still writes long hand, dresses from an archive of clothes he's owned since the 1980s, and refuses to have anything plastic, or anything from companies that mass produce, in the house. Right: A grid of framed Max Baur photographs lines a wall adjacent to Suzanne Fabry's 1934 painting entitled *The Three Graces*. A Gio Ponti sofa and an Alexandre Noll table sit on an André Arbus carpet. "Nothing really fits together here," says Joop. "On the other hand, it all seems quite happy here. As Nietzsche said, 'We have art so we don't perish from the truth.'"

WITH GRATITUDE to Maggie and James

ACKNOWLEDGMENTS

Heart and Home would not have been possible without many peoples' committed aesthetic and generosity. Thanks in particular to the inhabitants of every room featured and the photographers who brought their talent, passion, admiration, and fancy equipment to each location. Heartfelt thanks to Annie Kelly for her professional largesse and friendship; to Vicente Wolfe who set me on the road; to Haynes Llewellyn for unselfishly connecting dots; to Ricky Spears for his heart and sharp instincts. Special thanks to Barbara Bohl, John Ellis, Robin Holland, Laura Hull, Teresa Laughlin, Peter Murdock, Mark Roskams, and Yvette Renda for their support, and appreciation to Steve Blatz for his many talents. Thanks to the entire Rizzoli team, in particular Sandy Gilbert, and Ron Broadhurst for his steadfast support and sensibility. Last but not least, thanks to G.

PHOTOGRAPHY CREDITS

Antonio Pio Saracino—Peter Murdock

Brian McCarthy—Robin Holland

Calvin Tsao & Zack McKown—Peter Murdock

Deborah Ehrlich & Christopher Kurtz—Robin Holland

Ellen Johnson & Ronnie Schwartz—Mark Roskams

Federico de Vera—Robin Holland

George Lindemann—Mark Roskams

Gene Meyer & Frank de Biasi—Mark Roskams

Hanya Yanagihara—Peter Murdock

Haynes Llewellyn—Robin Holland

Hermes Mallea & Carey Maloney—Robin Holland

John Jay—Bruce Wolf, with the exception of pages 90 and 94, below, by Miles Johnson

Kelly Wearstler—Laura Hull

Kate Hume—Frans van der Heyden

Kenneth Cobonpue—Paolo Konst

Lee Ledbetter—Mark Roskams

Marjorie Skouras—Laura Hull

Paul Mathieu—Henry Wilson, with the exception of page 145, by Paul Mathieu

Paul Siskin—Robin Holland

Philip Michael Wolfson—Maxim Nilov

Ray Azoulay—Laura Hull

Rene Gonzalez—Mark Roskams

Robert Willson & David Serrano—John Ellis

Ronald Bricke—Peter Murdock

Ron Sharkey—Robin Holland

Scott Campbell—Peter Murdock

Shamir Shah & Malcolm Hill—Ellen Silverman

Thomas Lavin—John Ellis

Tom Pfeffer—Robin Holland

Wolfgang Joop—Beate Wätzel